A History of
English Country Sports

MICHAEL BILLETT

ROBERT HALE · LONDON

© *Michael Billett 1994*
First published in Great Britain 1994

ISBN 0 7090 5238 3

Robert Hale Limited
Clerkenwell House
Clerkenwell Green
London EC1R 0HT

2 4 6 8 10 9 7 5 3 1

The British Sporting Art Trust

The aim of the Trust, established as an independent charity in 1977, is to increase the appreciation of British sporting art which provides a unique chronicle of our sports, pastimes, and rural life over 300 years.

In partly achieving this aim, over fifty sporting works have been acquired for the Tate Gallery, London, through the Trust. These include a gift of thirty paintings from Mr Paul Mellon KBE and the Mrs F. Ambrose Clark Bequest. The Trust's Vestey Gallery of Sporting Art at Newmarket was opened in 1986 allowing annually changing exhibitions from the Trust's collections. A major extension to the Gallery in 1991 provided a print room and library, housing a comprehensive photographic collection including the B.S.A.T./Ackermann Archive from which many of the photographs in this book are taken.

Four exhibitions of twentieth-century sporting art have been mounted in London, Leicester, and one in Paris. *A Bibliography of British Sporting Artists* and *An Inventory of Sporting Art on Public Display in the United Kingdom* have been published, together with over twenty-five essays on sporting artists.

Grants have been made to the Fitzwilliam Museum; the Grosvenor Museum, Chester; Temple Newsam House, Leeds; and the Usher Gallery, Lincoln, to help them purchase sporting paintings. An annual sculpture prize is awarded and financial help given when possible to help young sporting artists with their studies.

The work of the Trust depends upon gifts, bequests, donations and subscriptions from members. The benefits to members include opportunities to visit private and public collections in the United Kingdom and abroad; invitations to private views and lectures; the receipt of newsletters and essays; attending occasional weekend symposiums on sporting art.

Anyone wishing to know more about the Trust and membership should write to: The Organizing Secretary B.S.A.T., 99 High Street, Newmarket, Suffolk CB8 8JL.

Registered Charity No. 274156

Photoset in Century Schoolbook by
Derek Doyle & Associates, Mold, Clwyd.
Printed and bound in Hong Kong by
Bookbuilders Limited.

Contents

List of Illustrations

[Name of artist and date of painting, where known, appears in brackets]

All illustrations courtesy of the B.S.A.T.

'Attila', a Bay Hunter,
with groom (*James
Seymour*)

Introduction

An inborn hunting instinct still resides in modern man. This is evidenced by the fact that the popularity of the pursuit of wild quarry by him has not apparently waned with the passage of time. Today, about five million people in Britain, from all walks of life, still show interest in country sports. It is estimated that a quarter of a million of these go, or follow, hunting in some form or another. The British Field Sports Society reports that approximately a million people turn out on Boxing Day to see Britain's hunts. It is also claimed that three million people still fish in our countryside and town waters. Three-quarters of a million indulge in various types of shooting. As well as the human involvement, about 20,000 hounds are owned by hunts and about 40,000 horses are kept for hunting.

This instinct to hunt was born of necessity in man's earlier evolutionary days. Hunting for food was essential for survival. Later, the poor poached for food to enliven their miserable existence, whilst kings and nobles hunted to obtain a welcome variation in their diet. The stag was the prime quarry, although boar in earlier days were also prized, and the art of falconry was developed to hunt smaller game. The introduction of harsh Forest and Game Laws protected the game and reserved it as the exclusive right of the nobility and wealthy.

Throughout the centuries, the Royals have given their patronage to all country field sports, especially those using hawk, horse and hound in the pursuit of wild game. From the Norman Conquest to the eighteenth century, the nobility predominantly favoured the deer. They paid little attention to the hunting of non-edible pests, such as the otter and fox. This was generally left to persons of lower social rank. However, during the last two centuries, the hunting of the fox has received increasing royal support as a field sport, particularly in recent years by HRH Prince Charles. The decline in the deer population in the late seventeeth century, predominantly brought about by woodland clearance, accelerated the interest of the Royals in alternative country sports. These included, as well as fox hunting, hare hunting, shooting and game-fishing.

The Duke of Portland
on 'Cockney'
(*James Seymour*)

The coursing of hares to test the speed of greyhounds also became a popular pastime, in addition to the hunting of the hare on horse or on foot with hounds. The development of the sporting gun in the seventeenth century brought about the birth of estate shooting of partridge, pheasant and grouse. The wealthy also enjoyed fishing for the game-fish, salmon and trout. With the passage of time, angling became one of the most popular countryside pastimes. The poorer members of society took up coarse fishing for sport, the fish when caught on the hook being returned to the water. This particular form of fishing has, in recent years, given rise to varying opinions on the cruelty of the sport. The fish was not caught for food or because it was a pest; it was done purely as a pastime and it was feasible that the same fish may have been hooked several times. Game-fishing also presented a point on ethics because of the lengthy time it may have taken to run or fight a fish after it had been hooked and before it was brought to the net.

Many of the nobility and richer landowners delighted in having pictures of hunting scenes and their favourite hunters hanging on the walls of their palaces and great houses. This fashion started in the seventeenth century. Many famous painters specialized in this sporting art field. The father of English sporting pictures was Francis Barlow. His drawings for his book *The Severall Ways of Hunting, Hawking and Fishing in the Englishway* were etched by Hollar and date from 1671.

John Wootton quickly followed and he painted many sporting and hunting pictures for both George I and George II, as well as many other members of the nobility. George Stubbs, born in 1724, became probably the greatest of all sporting artists and produced a prolific number of works. John Nott Sartorius and James Seymour also painted many hunting scenes in the eighteenth century.

Ben Marshall in the late eighteenth and early nineteenth centuries attended many hunt meetings and quickly gained a reputation for his sporting paintings, as also did James Pollard, who in addition became the leading coaching artist of the day. Henry Thomas Alken, in the first half of the nineteenth century, produced an enormous number of etchings and sporting art pictures. John Frederick Herring (senior), John Ferneley (senior) and Sir Francis Grant in the same century became famous for their hunting and racing paintings. Sir Alfred Munnings carried on the tradition well into the twentieth century but became better known for his paintings of thoroughbred horses than for his hunting scenes.

Despite the pleasurable scenes depicted in most of the paintings, our ancestors also indulged in many unpleasant and cruel activities. These were committed against both man and animals. In the more distant past, our forefathers were particularly adept at devising unpleasant ways of killing or humiliating their fellow-beings. Crucifixion, burning at the stake, hanging-drawing-and-quartering and beheading were a few accepted methods. Later, less drastic ordeals were torture, ducking stools, the use of the pillory, stocks and treadmills, together with flogging and the cat o'nine tails. Many of these took place in public and were used as spectacles and entertainments, often on public holidays.

It is perhaps not surprising, therefore, that man thought little of the appalling distress caused to animals by the many baiting sports which were also practised for entertainment. Barbaric blood sports involving the baiting of bears, bulls and badgers became extremely popular, together with cock-fighting. Broken-down horses were baited with dogs, although in general horses were not considered aggressive enough for baiting sports. Gambling fuelled many of these cruel activities, as both rich and poor wagered for excitement. Unlike the earlier days of hunting, there was no great class barrier between the people who followed such callous pursuits. It must be borne in

mind, in the social context, that there were few alternative entertainments available for the majority of the population.

Fox with Pheasant and Terriers Watching (*George Armfield*)

Several less well-known country sports developed in the eighteenth century. One of the more ghastly but popular was the rural sport of goose-riding. This was not peculiar to any season, festival or holiday but was done purely for fun, entertainment and no doubt wagering. Firstly, the participants thoroughly greased the neck of the unfortunate live goose. They then hung it upside down with its feet tied to the bough of a tree, or to a line stretched at a convenient height between two stakes. The contestants, in turn, rode on horseback at speed and attempted to grab the goose by its slippery neck. The object was to snatch the neck from the body, as they galloped past without decreasing pace.

Many taverns in the eighteenth century provided other so-called rough sports, such as dog fighting, pond duck hunting and terrier rat catching contests, as well as the more common bear and bull baiting and cock-fighting. A pub sign such as the 'Dog and Duck' indicated it had a pond at the back where customers could wager whether their dog could successfully catch a duck thrown onto the water. The inn sign normally pictured a spaniel with a duck in its mouth. A pub name such as the 'Dog and Bear' showed that bear baiting took place on the premises, while the fighting cocks clearly illustrated the sport available, either inside or outside in the backyard. Pubs gradually grew as centres for many other sports, including the racing of whippets against rabbits and later as headquarters for many angling clubs. The local hostelry often became the meeting point for the hunt members before their departure in search of the fox. Before setting out, they fortified themselves with a strong drink from the traditional stirrup cup.

From the early to the mid-eighteenth century, hunting, shooting and fishing became the principal interest of the majority of landowners. They started to spend more of their time in the countryside, rather than undertaking journeys abroad or staying in their town houses. When hunting purely for food became of less importance to them, various rules were introduced to make the sport more skilful and difficult. Also, the quarry was given a sporting chance to escape. The quarry was either killed or escaped unharmed. Later, the true sportsman developed, who considered it inhumane for a hunter only to wound an animal and let it escape to die in distress. The need to avoid unnecessary suffering therefore became important. Ironically, the same humanity did not apply to any poor poacher caught in the act, as penalties were extremely harsh and little mercy was shown. Later, the richer Victorians took great pride in the country estates they purchased with their newly acquired wealth. They visited them as often as possible to escape the smoke and dirt of the Industrial Revolution.

Much of the English countryside that is enjoyed today has been fashioned by the influence of country field sports. This started with the establishment of the royal hunting forests. In addition, many of the small woods, coverts and hedgerows which exist today were planted, more than two hundred years ago, to give cover to foxes, partridges and pheasants. At the same time they gave and still give shelter to many other wild creatures and birds. Many moorlands of heather in the north of England and also Scotland have been preserved and managed purely to encourage the survival of grouse. They provide also an extensive unpolluted habitat for a variety of wildlife.

Many of the saltmarshes and intertidal mudflats on our estuaries are havens for a multitude of migratory wildfowl. Strangely, much of

Snipe in the Marshes
(*William Hollywood*)

their preservation has been due to the effort of wildfowl shooters, as the participants in the sport have kept saltmarsh grass under management and prevented the spread of other invasive grasses into it. They have also kept expanses of water open. Birds such as wigeon feed on the saltmarsh grasses. In addition, much of the pressure for good river management has been brought by anglers and their desire for fish to survive in our rivers and streams. Uncontaminated rivers ensure that river plant life and insects prosper, as well as the fish. Unfortunately, much of today's river contamination stems from accidental leakages from silage pits and agricultural sprays carried by the wind.

A strange paradoxical relationship therefore exists between country field sports and the conservation of the extremely varied English landscape and its wildlife. This is partly explained by the fact that only a tiny percentage of the countryside enjoys protection as a nature reserve. Landowners and farmers control nearly ninety per cent of the land. They care for it so that it is improved when handed over to their descendants. If their general support for field sports and the maintenance of natural cover for wildlife were withdrawn, then farming might become even more intensive and the countryside would change further. The use of large machines for modern efficient food production has already drastically reduced the number of hedgerows and woods to a fraction of their total of fifty years ago.

Some farmers are now trying to rectify the situation by leaving small areas of their fields uncultivated to encourage and nurture wildlife. Recent European Community legislation has also indirectly contributed to this aim. The spraying of agricultural chemicals and pesticides interferes with the delicate balance of nature. Nature has always been cruel, as the population of any species is determined by its available food source. This may be grazing land, or the availability of smaller animals for predators to hunt. When food is short only the stronger of the species survive; the others starve. The loss of natural habitats, together with chemical pollution, have significantly reduced populations of otters, badgers, hares and birds of prey.

These diverse factors influence wildlife population and present a greater hazard to the future conservation of wildlife than country field sports. Centuries of hunting for sport seldom led to the extinction of a species; it would obviously be counter-productive to let that happen. However, the pursuit of wild quarry, by horse and hound, remains a highly emotive and controversial issue. Many of the arguments are due to misunderstanding and lack of communication between people who live in urban societies and those who reside in the countryside. Knowledge provides the fuel for debate and this is essential to enable a dispassionate judgement.

A photograph in a newspaper of a stag being 'bayed' by hounds infuriates a city dweller. Quite rightly so when viewed in isolation, and it is only natural to pity the plight of the individual stag. However, the strange fact remains that the herds of red deer on Exmoor would now probably be extinct without the hunting of them. Farmers would not have tolerated the damage caused by them to their crops on unfenced Exmoor. The deer would have either been completely eliminated by shooting or killed by poachers, if they had not been conserved and protected by the local farmers for sport. Shooting at long range by an inexperienced shot, or a poacher using the wrong type of weapon or a lurcher dog, would be even more cruel. The deer would not be shot at close range and killed instantly, as occurs after it is surrounded and 'bayed' by hounds during a stag hunt. Even if it were possible to fence Exmoor and stag hunting were prohibited, a selective cull would still have to be made to maintain a healthy herd and prevent starvation.

No deer now live on neighbouring Dartmoor, as no conservation for hunting took place there in the past. They were eliminated by the farmers. Those they could not kill themselves were exterminated, at their request, by the Duke of Bedford's staghounds towards the end of the eighteenth century. It is therefore essential in a modern society to strike the correct balance between preservation and acceptable damage to crops and property.

Deer have no natural predators in England since the extinction of the wolf many years ago, so man has to assume this role to preserve a healthy wild population that can be sustained by the local environment. For example, if a deer herd was left alone in the wild it

Foxes with a Dead Chicken (*Charles Clowes*)

could increase its numbers by up to one-third each year; hence a selective culling is essential.

The Royal Society for the Prevention of Cruelty to Animals (RSPCA) agrees that culling is necessary but favours the use of highly skilled marksmen to shoot selected animals with a rifle. It is opposed to the hunting of any animal with hounds. The RSPCA emphasises that the West Country stag-hunting packs kill only approximately 120 animals each year, compared with a thousand red deer culled by shooting in England and Scotland. Stag hunting with hounds is illegal in Scotland, mainly because of its accent on game preservation and sheep breeding. The New Forest buckhounds take approximately ten fallow bucks each year but three hundred to four hundred bucks and hinds are shot. The hunting of deer takes place with staghounds possessing more stamina than speed, which usually means the chase continues for several hours. The RSPCA views this as particularly cruel, as deer are prone to fall victim to myopathy, an often fatal condition caused by stress.

The National Trust adopts a different attitude. It allows deer hunting with hounds on its land, as it was concluded after a two-year research inquiry that it was of 'critical importance' for the welfare of the red deer and the preservation of its habitat. However, the Trust has set up a further research programme to study in more detail the lives and habitats of the red deer in Somerset and Devon, together with their conservation and management. Both pro-hunt and anti-hunt lobbies are contributing towards the study.

The fox presents a different problem. It is treated by the countryman as a pure agricultural pest but one wonderfully gifted to adapt to changing circumstances in its search for food. On farmland, the fox remains a beautiful but vicious killer. It attacks lambs, chickens and game-birds. The danger to chickens is no longer so great as it was in the past, owing to the reduction in the number of free-range birds. The problem of foxes attacking lambs may be slightly exaggerated. Many of the small lambs found savaged may have already died before being found by the fox, a well-known scavenger. It is certainly true that the fox may select an extremely weak, or injured, small lamb for a meal and it is indisputable that foxes greatly harass flocks of sheep and lambs.

In addition, many urban populations of foxes have now developed when previously they were only found in the countryside. It is estimated that the country sustains a population in excess of two hundred thousand foxes, so without control the nuisance factor could become intolerable, especially in certain farming areas. In fact, farmers and gamekeepers kill about eight times as many foxes by shooting and snaring than are killed by registered packs of foxhounds. The question therefore arises of the best and most humane method of control – the alternative methods are poisoning, gassing, shooting, trapping or hunting.

Poisoning kills other wildlife and is not now an acceptable legal option. The sustained gassing of foxes in their earths, most of which are known, would no doubt virtually eliminate them from an area but also presents a hazard to other wildlife. Shooting at long range is extremely difficult and often the fox is only wounded. However, if foxes prove a problem most farmers resort to this method.

Gin traps are now illegal. These were snares which tightened each time the animal moved and caused much agony. Modern free-running snares which hold but do not tighten, keep the animal captive until a gamekeeper arrives to shoot it in the snare. Unfortunately, other animals can also be accidentally trapped. The traditional hunting of foxes by hounds ensures that the fox is either killed or it escapes unharmed. In this case, the question arises of the possible terror it may encounter during the chase.

In 1949 the Government set up the Scott Henderson Committee to study the issue of 'Cruelty to Wild Animals'. The intensive study over a two-year period included hunting and considered the most humane way of controlling foxes, if their numbers need be restricted. The fox, like the deer, has no natural predators. The Committee, under the chairmanship of J. Scott Henderson KC, included veterinary surgeons, zoologists and naturalists among its members. They concluded, in 1951, that traditional hunting was the least cruel of the alternative culling methods. This was the most detailed investigation that has ever been held on the subject.

Many dispute these findings and many attempts have since been made to abolish hunting. The anti-hunt movement views the sport as cruel and elitist, as well as inflicting exhaustion, terror and trauma on the victim. The latest private member's bill to ban hunting was narrowly defeated in Parliament in 1992. The anti-hunting case has been eloquently and well presented over the years, mainly through Parliament, by the efforts of The League Against Cruel Sports. This is done chiefly by lobbying Members of Parliament, local councillors and political parties with relevant information supporting their case. The organization was founded about seventy years ago to campaign for the protection of all British wild animals from cruelty. It now owns about 2500 acres of sanctuary in the West Country; most of its land purchases are in areas where animals are still hunted. The League Against Cruel Sports works towards its goal of making the hunting of wildlife with packs of hounds, in the name of sport, illegal.

A few members of various other animal rights, anti-bloodsports and hunt saboteurs' associations sometimes indulge in unlawful activities and lose much essential public goodwill for their cause. There is a lawful right to hunt and equally the saboteurs possess a

Fox leaving Earth
(*George Armfield*)

perfectly legal right to demonstrate peacefully. The hunt never rides over private land without the owner's permission but the saboteurs often trespass to impede the hunt. Controversy arises and sometimes violence, when they refuse to leave. Despite these incidents, The Hunt Saboteurs' Association, founded in the 1960s, believes in non-violent direct action in the hunting field. The Association works against all sports which it views as cruel to wildlife and these now include the hunting of foxes, deer, hares, mink, as well as hare coursing, game-shooting and angling.

Tactics used by anti-hunt campaigners include the blowing of hunting horns to confuse the hounds and create general havoc. They also distract hounds by playing tapes of hounds in full cry over a megaphone and by imitating the voice calls of the huntsman. Any actions taken which result in horses 'bolting' are obviously extremely dangerous, not only to both horse and rider but also to members of the public. Hunt saboteurs also lay aniseed-based or other types of chemical trail to mislead the hounds into following a false scent.

The debate on hunting will no doubt continue. This may be influenced, in the future, by EC legislation which may materialize on the conservation of wildlife and its habitats. Let us hope that the fox will always be respected as a tolerable pest as nature intended. It would be a terrible shame if such an intriguing animal was virtually eliminated from the countryside by a sustained campaign of gassing, snaring or shooting at some time in the future – ironically, methods thought by the Scott Henderson Committee to be less humane than hunting with hounds. In hunting, the fox is normally killed instantly by a bite to the neck by one leading hound. It is a popular misconception that the fox is torn to pieces by the hounds before it is dead. Some people in favour of hunting argue that hunting of the fox has prevented its extinction. The fox-hunter likes to maintain a healthy but controlled population for sport and obviously has no wish to exterminate the fox from the countryside.

The League Against Cruel Sports takes the view that hunting with hounds is done purely for sport, with no effective contribution to pest control. The League believes that the fox is not a significant pest to farmers and if left alone, the foxes would balance their numbers by the food availability in their defended territory. This concept is true for most animals but it is difficult to envisage the farming community allowing the fox to run unmolested near their stock or game.

However, if the hunting of the fox is to continue it must always be carried out meticulously to the current rules laid down by the Masters of Foxhounds Association. The hunting community still suffer bad publicity following the early 1990s Quorn Hunt scandal when a private video, released by The League Against Cruel Sports, showed members breaking rules on the killing of a fox. The malpractice led to senior hunt officials being suspended. This incident lost much public goodwill and did little to enhance general support for fox-hunting. In 1993, further bad publicity was given to fox-hunting by the Beaufort Hunt using illegal materials for stopping badger sett entrances, in contravention of the Protection of Badgers Act 1992. This resulted in The National Trust banning the Beaufort Hunt from fox-hunting on their land.

Nowadays, the cost of maintaining hunters, especially in time of recession, has become fairly prohibitive. This could affect the sport by forcing members reluctantly to abandon their expensive pastime. A season's hunting in the fashionable shires now costs a considerable amount of money. Some hunts also incur the expense of hiring private security stewards and the police often have to be brought in to prevent public disorder. The police attempt to placate situations because trespass is only a civil offence and they are relatively powerless over hunt protesters. They can only ask anti-hunt saboteurs to leave or escort them off private property. Landowners and the pro-field sports lobby are seeking stronger legislation to make it a criminal offence to trespass with intent to disrupt a legal activity, such as hunting, shooting and fishing. However, this type of new legislation would not be welcomed by the ramblers, in case their activities also became curtailed.

Fox-hunting has survived many obstacles in the past, and this centuries-old tradition of the English countryside will continue, as long as it is legally entitled to do so by Parliament. However, tradition alone will not be a valid enough reason for the continuance of the sport in a modern society. Many former blood sports were traditional but this did not prevent their eventual ban. The welfare of the animals and the countryside they inhabit must be the first priority. If the overall welfare demands a control of a particular species then the most humane method of culling must be the correct way, whether this is by shooting, hunting or whatever other means. The future for field sports as a culling method therefore depends on their acceptance by the general public as humane. Most people would agree that the killing of animals, or birds, purely for human entertainment would not be an adequate reason for any sport to continue into the twenty-first century.

Finally, most people who ride to hounds do so for the excitement of riding at speed across country. If a ban on hunting with hounds materializes in the future, let us hope that their pleasure may still be fulfilled by the packs turning to 'drag hunting'. In this, the hounds follow an artificial scent, rather than that of a live quarry. If not, the question will have to be faced of what to do with the twenty thousand hounds kept by the various hunts. They have always lived as a pack in kennels and are not domesticated. The other decision to be made will be which culling method to use instead of hunting.

A Bulldog
(*J.F. Herring, Sen.*)

1   Bear, Bull and Badger Baiting and Rough Sports

The barbaric baiting of bears with dogs, as a sporting entertainment, was very popular in England and retained this public support from the Middle Ages to the early nineteenth century. The Italians may have first introduced it into England during the reign of King John in the thirteenth century. It appears extremely likely that most of the bears for the sport were imported into Britain for this particular purpose, because bears in the wild did not survive in England after about the tenth century. Also, it is extremely unlikely that wild bears ever existed in Ireland, so the bears used probably came from Europe or further afield.

In addition to their misuse for baiting purposes, it is worth recalling that many bears were killed to produce the much acclaimed bear grease. This was extremely popular as a hair restorative product and dressing from the twelfth century to the end of the Victorian era. Presumably, it was thought that as bears never went bald, so the grease would be effective in promoting vigorous hair growth when rubbed into the human scalp. It was usually spread thickly on the head to keep the hair tidy, especially when the fashion of wearing wigs declined. It was considered by many that the grease from the Russian black bear was the supreme product. Many thousands of bears from Russia were therefore killed to satisfy this demand in England and other European countries. Ceramic bear grease pot lids, showing the manufacturers' names from the Victorian period, may still be found in our antique shops today. Many more bears died for their bear grease than were ever killed by baiting.

Bears were considered ideal animals for baiting because of their size and aggressive nature when attacked. They had powerful limbs and long curved claws, and could stand upright on their hind legs. They enjoyed a keen sense of smell and were very intelligent but had the disadvantages of poor hearing and eyesight. They could be tamed and controlled by man and led on a chain. The dogs used in the baiting were of the mastiff type and some may have been descendants of the earlier dog breeds used to hunt wild boars in the Norman forests.

The official post of Royal Bearward, or Ursarius, was created in 1484, when Richard III, in his first year as King, appointed John Browne to the office. The post became part of the royal household and it seems it carried no direct remuneration. However, the Royal Bearward employed under-officers, called 'Keepers of Bears and Mastiffs', who received pay from the treasurer on the Council's warrant. The post of Royal Bearward remained part of the royal household for many years and carried on throughout the Elizabethan reign. Most nobles had their own bearwards and after the fifteenth century allowed them to undertake commercial ventures with their bears at manors outside their own.

The peak of popularity for bear baiting was reached in Tudor times. Henry VIII, like his predecessors, appointed his own Royal Bearward, whose sole task was to look after the king's bears and dogs. As well as attending to the bear pits in the Courts where the king's bears may appear, the Royal Bearward also arranged matches in the royal parks. These private affairs were especially used to entertain visiting nobility. He also licensed John Cooper to arrange some public animal baits.

Queen Mary was also entertained by bear baiting when visiting her half-sister, Elizabeth, at Hatfield House. It was quite usual at the time to have a mixture of baitings, plays and singing. Elizabeth, when she became queen, continued her enthusiasm for bear baiting. This lasted well into her reign and it was reported that in 1575, she much enjoyed the lavish entertainment laid on for her by one of her favourites, the Earl of Leicester at Kenilworth Castle. This included the spectacle of a pack of dogs being allowed to attack thirteen bears which were chained up in the inner court of the house. This type of amusement was still much used to entertain visiting ambassadors and diplomats as well as nobility. The sight of blood and gore delighted and thrilled them. Bear baits were especially popular with the Royals during Christmas holidays and Whitsuntide, the bears and dogs being brought to the Court wherever it might be in the country.

In Elizabethan times, it was a more unusual entertainment to pit men against the bear. In this contest, about half-a-dozen men, equipped with whips, would surround the bear which was securely fastened with a chain; the bear was sometimes even blinded. The men would then attempt to whip the bear into a frenzy by lashing it unmercifully. The bear would try to defend itself by grabbing its tormentors, or sometimes snatching the whips from their hands. Men were often badly injured and slashed with the claws if they were not agile enough to dodge the bear's clutches and blows. One particular famous blind bear was 'Harry Hunks' and he became a great favourite owing to his many successes in baiting contests.

The post of the Master of Bears had now been created as a Crown Office and this carried a stipend of sixteen pence a day. His responsibility was to ensure that a supply of bears was available at all times, and he was paid out of the Queen's Treasury. The Master of Bears also had the power to commandeer any dogs which he thought would be suitable for baiting purposes. His staff scoured the country for promising dogs to press into royal service and train. One enterprising Master of Bears appears also to have capitalized on the great popularity of the baiting sports, for on 11th October 1561, Sir Saunders Duncombe was granted a patent for 'the sole profit of the fighting and combating of wild and domestic beasts in England for the space of fourteen years'. It would appear unlikely that his patent right was strictly enforced but if it had been, the gentleman would have died a very rich man from his accrued earnings, over the years, from such a popular sport.

Just before this patent expired, another was granted to Ralph Bowes on 2nd June 1573, as the new Master of Bears. This stated the post as 'the room or office of Chief Master Overseer and Ruler of all and singular our game pastimes and sports, that is to say of all and every our bears, bulls and mastiff dogs'. Other holders of the appointment of Master of Bears were Cuthbert Vaughan and Sir Richard Long. They all possessed the sole right of baiting the royal bears.

James I when he came to the throne experimented with a different and particularly dangerous form of baiting; this was with the lions which were traditionally kept at the Tower of London. Several baitings took place there during the first decade of the seventeenth century, under the supervision of the Master of the Bears at that time, Edward Alleyn. He was a well-known former actor and he made a considerable profit from his new post. Alleyn, together with Henslowe of the Rose Theatre, were joint patent holders of the 'Royal Game of Bears, Bulls and Mastiff Dogs'. In the venture with the lions, the dogs proved no match for the beasts which were quite wild but in one encounter a dog survived. It was nursed back to health and then well-cared for. The *Morning Herald* that was published at the time quoted Prince Henry, the son of James I, as saying, 'he that had fought with the King of beasts should never after fight an inferior creature'.

There are no records to suggest other lion baits until about two hundred years later, in 1825, when an entrepreneur revived them. They were arranged at Warwick on the road leading to Northampton, at a site called 'Old Factory Yard'. The baits were staged in a cage approximately fifteen feet square. It was raised about five feet off the ground to offer better viewing facilities for the paying spectators. The space between the bars of the cage was sufficient for the dogs to enter, after they had walked up a ramp to reach the cage. The lions owned by the entrepreneur were tame and well-fed. They made no real effort to bite, or kill, the dogs when they entered the cage. A total of six dogs was used, released two at a time. The dogs seized the lion by the nose or its lips, but the lion protected itself only by knocking the dogs aside with its paws. The contests incensed many people who thought it extremely cruel to bait tame lions. The baits often ended with the dogs injured and the lion exhausted by the attacks. A further series of lion baits which were arranged brought more critical comment in *The Times*.

To return to the subject of bear baiting, the unfortunate animal was tethered by a chain around its neck or leg to a tree, if the contest was to take place in a private park. However, it became more common to chain the bear to a stake placed in the middle of a specially built bear pit or ring. These later developed a theatre-like appearance and were known as beargardens. They were noted for their rowdy and noisy scenes. In the bait, four to six mastiffs were generally let loose as a pack to attack the bear. It was not unusual for two of the dogs to be immediately killed or badly injured. These were replaced by the unleashing of fresh dogs and the fight continued until the dogs were defeated, or the bear became so injured it could no longer defend itself. Dogs were considered expendable but bears were much more valuable and were seldom allowed to be killed. The bearward liked to save them to fight another day.

The bears were well looked after out of the ring, despite the terrible ordeal they were forced to suffer in it. The bearward dressed their wounds and cared for their general welfare, bedding and food. He also travelled and accompanied the bears when they were transported for baiting matches to different parts of the country. When in a strange town or village, the bears were often paraded through the streets by the bearward to advertise that a programme of baiting was to take place. Sometimes a monkey rode on the back of the bear, and the procession along the roads was often accompanied by singing and dancing minstrels. On occasions, the bearward would even take his favourite bear on a chain into a tavern for a drink of water or something stronger. One famous bear, called 'Old Nell', from Middlewich in Cheshire, always loved to have several pints of beer with his handler after a bait. 'Old Nell' gained the reputation of being a great killer of dogs in the baiting arena. Bearwards also taught some bears to do tricks to amuse the crowds. Performing bears became a familiar and popular sight in the streets, especially during the reign of Elizabeth I. The bears were always muzzled and many were trained to dance.

Eventually, nearly every town and large village had its own official bearward and pack of dogs. The possession of a really good bear was a matter of great local pride. Famous fighting bears like 'Harry Hunks', the 'Great Sackerson', 'Ned Whiting' and 'George Stone' became national heroes. 'George Stone' was sadly missed after being killed in a bait held before the King of Denmark in 1606. The dogs were usually housed and chained in wooden kennels adjoining the beargarden. They were too savage to keep in any other way. Sunday became the popular day for bear baiting, although much later, in the reign of James I, it was discouraged on Sundays. In fact, James I supported the sport and was enthusiastic about it on all other days of the week.

In London, the most famous beargarden was the Paris Garden which received much royal patronage. This was built in 1526, at Bankside on the south of the River Thames in Southwark, behind the site where Shakespeare's Globe Theatre was later built in 1599. It was situated just west of Southwark Cathedral. It provided accommodation for about a thousand spectators and was designed in the form of a circular three-storey-high amphitheatre with huge scaffolding stands. The basic price of an entrance ticket was initially one penny but an extra penny was payable to secure one of the better viewing positions on the scaffolding or in an area of less congested standing. The arena was used exclusively for bear baiting but in about 1570, a further circus-type arena was erected on adjacent land for the rival sport of bull baiting. In its prime period, the Paris Garden housed about twenty bears, three bulls and about a hundred mastiffs. The ratio of bears to bulls shows the relative popularity of the two sports at this time in London.

Although injuries were sometimes caused to spectators by the occasional escape of a bear or savage mastiff, the greatest tragedy at the Paris Garden occurred at 4 pm on Sunday 13th January, 1583. The arena was so packed with spectators that one of the wooden stands collapsed. In the ensuing panic, five men and two women died and about one hundred and fifty were injured. Some claimed it was an 'Act of God' for holding such an event on a Sunday. However, the Paris Garden soon recovered from the shock and it was rebuilt as a three-storey amphitheatre which was managed by Henslowe of the Rose Theatre. It continued as a popular venue for baiting. However, Thursday became the established day for the sport rather than the Sabbath. In 1584, it was recorded that a variation on the normal baiting procedures took place there. It seems that the dogs were first unleashed on a fairly small bear as an appetizer. When this preliminary fight was over, the dogs that survived had to face immediately a medium-sized bear, which was introduced into the arena. If the dogs still survived, a third huge bear was pitted against

JIM

them, to the great delight and amusement of the audience. Another deviation to entertain the crowd was to let loose into the arena a pony with a monkey tied to its back. The inevitable attack of the mastiffs on the pony, together with the shrieks of the terrified monkey, were thought to be great fun. The people thought little of the cruelty, for

'Jim', a Bull Terrier
(*Cecil Aldin*)

they themselves lived in harsh and bloody times.

Gradually, towards the end of the sixteenth century, the growing popularity of the early theatres and play-going created competition to bear baiting. To counteract this, it became common to hold both plays and baitings at the same venue. The baiting sport usually took place before the play commenced. Later, separate days for the two activities became more common. This shift in public taste was accommodated by the demolition of the main buildings at the Paris Garden in about 1614. A new dual-purpose theatre called The Hope was constructed in its place. This new building staged plays, as well as baiting contests. The stage could be raised or taken down depending upon the requirement. The Hope was also fitted with a central opening for free ventilation, to get rid of the smell of the bears and dogs. Initially, an agreement was reached to allow one day for bear baiting each fortnight. Later, a routine became established of staging plays on Mondays, Wednesdays, Fridays and Saturdays, with bear baiting on Tuesdays and Thursdays. Other theatres on the south bank of the Thames, such as The Swan and The Rose, were also circular in shape and held both baitings and plays. The Rose was first built in about 1587 and was of timber-framed construction with a thatched roof. It was possibly octagonal in shape. The use of a thatched roof appears surprising as thatch was officially banned on new buildings in London from 1212.

The Puritans detested bear baiting and the other baiting sports, not out of sympathy for the plight of the animals but for the morally degrading effect they thought it was having on the people. Macaulay in his *History of England* suggested: 'The Puritans hated bear baiting not because it gave pain to the bear, but because it gave pleasure to the spectators.' Eventually, the Puritans' views prevailed and the baiting of bears was officially prohibited by an order of the Long Parliament in 1642. However, despite this ban, the popularity remained so strong that the order was largely ignored and it continued at The Hope until 1655. Even then, it could only be stopped by sending a company of soldiers to The Hope to shoot the bears. This was done on Saturday 9th February, 1655 by the order of Thomas Pride, who at the time was the Sheriff of Surrey. The site was then re-developed for tenement building.

During the Restoration period, bear baiting was revived by King Charles II as a sporting entertainment and it remained well supported throughout the whole of the eighteenth century. An attempt to ban bear baiting and also bull baiting was made again at the beginning of the nineteenth century. However, the House of Commons rejected the bill. It was re-introduced and the second reading stage was reached on 24th May 1802. This was defeated by a majority of thirteen votes, despite support for the bill by such notable politicians as Sheridan and Wilberforce. The House was swayed by a passionate speech made by the Honourable William Wyndham, who convinced Parliament that the bill had been introduced purely as a plot, inspired by Jacobeans and Methodists, to destroy the traditional English way of life. He argued as if the British Constitution must stand or fall with the fate of the beargarden. Other bills to ban bear baiting and similar activities were brought over the following years. In fact, eleven different bills were unsuccessfully presented to Parliament between 1800 and 1835. It was difficult to ban cruel sports at this period of history. However, this must be put into the context of the times, for man was still cruel to his fellow man in the early nineteenth century. For example, slavery had not been abolished throughout Britain's colonial empire. The Honourable William Wyndham, although in favour of the continuation of traditional English sports, such as animal baiting, fought with equal zeal in the House of Commons for the suppression of the slave trade, which he found completely abhorrent. Eventually, in 1835 a bill became law which finally made bear, bull and badger baiting illegal. The bill also banned the sports of dog-fighting and cock-fighting in England. Despite the official ban, illegal baits still took place. For example, records show that one was held, just after 1835, at Wirksworth in Derbyshire. Other illegal baits were staged at Eccles in 1842 and at West Derby, in Lancashire, in 1853. There must have been many others that were never recorded.

The history of the rival sport of bull baiting can be traced back to 1209. The idea probably started when William, the Earl of Warren, looked out of his window one day and saw a large mastiff dog, belonging to the butcher, barking and attacking one of the two bulls in the meadow. Some reports suggest that the bull was also owned by the butcher. In its panic the bull broke out of the field and was hotly pursued down the road into the town of Stamford in Lincolnshire by the dog. The Earl thought the spectacle was highly amusing and followed behind on horseback. Later, he decided it would make a great entertainment for the townsfolk. He therefore set aside a meadow and decided to hold a bull bait as an annual event. This was on condition that the butchers in the town would select one ferocious or mad bull each year and donate the animal for the fight against the dogs. The event traditionally took place six weeks before Christmas.

Variations on the initial theme evolved and the annual Stamford bull-run became established. The night before the event the selected bull was kept in a stall by the aldermen of the town. The residents were warned to secure their doors and windows. Then each year, on thirteenth November, the bull was turned loose, after a bell was rung at about 10.45 am to warn children and the infirm off the streets. The bull was first released into one street only, which had been barricaded with wagons to prevent the bull's escape. The people liked to tease and make it angry before the run commenced. They hurled missiles at it and tried other ways to irritate the animal. For example, a man would knock out the ends of a hogshead cask then climb into it. The crowd would roll the cask at the bull to tempt it to try the near impossible task of tossing it. The barrel would always roll away and the man inside remained relatively secure. When the bull was considered mad enough, the barricades were removed and the bull driven out to roam the streets. The bull was then pursued not just by dogs but also by the local inhabitants who chased the bull through the town, after first arming themselves with clubs and staves. The tradition was that the clubs must be made of wood and no

Two Terriers and a
Rat in a Trap
(*Charles Towne*)

iron parts were to be added to them.

The idea of the bull-run was to force the bull onto the town bridge, where it would either be driven off into the fields beyond or heaved over the bridge into the water. The latter course of action demanded considerable courage on behalf of the men. If the bull fell into the water, it would try to escape over the meadows. These were very marshy during November and the resulting muddy ground entailed much so-called fun as the bull would often slip, together with its pursuers. Sometimes the pursuit lasted all day and it only ended when the bull or its tormentors were exhausted. The animal was eventually surrounded by the men and callously clubbed to death. The carcass was sold cheaply to the lower classes. Alternatively, a feast was organized for the poor, after the bull had been roasted. The people who had participated in the chase then voted to decide who had been the most courageous during the day's event. He was rewarded with a special part of the animal, aptly named the 'Great Gut'.

In 1788, the Mayor of Stamford and Lord Exeter tried to end the annual event but their efforts proved unsuccessful. Lord Exeter lived at Burleigh House, close to Stamford. The Mayor employed some dragoons to halt the event and they intercepted the bull-run at St George's Gate in the town. However, the officer in charge of the dragoons refused to stop it on the grounds that the people were only peacefully walking on the public highway. He dismissed the troops and to the annoyance of the Mayor, they joined in the bull-run themselves. Riots erupted in 1833 and 1836, when further attempts to stop it were made by The Society for the Prevention of Cruelty to Animals. Their representatives were forced to depart in haste. In 1837, the Society brought charges against several men for their role in the previous year's event. This action met with little success. The Home Secretary then ordered the town officials to take stronger action to force a ban. The local magistrates swore in several special constables from the town but all they were willing to do was to protect property. They refused to stop the bull-run and some even participated in it.

In 1838, a mixture of soldiers and police from outside the town were brought in to halt the chase of the bull through the streets but again their efforts were frustrated. Despite locating all the bulls in the town the day before, then locking them up and guarding them, one still mysteriously appeared. It was rumoured it had been smuggled in by a certain noble lord from his nearby estate in a wagon. The following year, in desperation a posse of forty-three dragoons, twenty metropolitan police and about ninety local constables was formed to stop the same thing happening again but with no success, as another bull was smuggled in. In 1840 the local people agreed by their own decision to abandon the custom, as they decided that the annual event was just causing more trouble than it was worth. No doubt their decision was influenced by the fact that their rates had been increased by sixpence in the pound to pay for the cost of extra police and military intervention.

Another more cruel type of bull-run took place annually at Tutbury in Staffordshire and it dated back to the fourteeth century, the time of John of Gaunt. The event was known as 'The Minstrels Bull-Running', the Minstrels being the name of an early form of local guild in the Middle Ages. They performed the musical entertainment at Tutbury Castle and elected their own 'King of Music'. The proceedings always took place on 16th August, on the morning of the Feast of Assumption. The Prior of Tutbury arranged for a bull to be taken to the Abbey gate where it was prepared for the day's amusement. The horrific preparation took the form of cutting off the bull's ears, horns and tail. Its body was then smeared with soap to make it difficult to hold, and pepper was blown up its nose. The enraged and terrified creature was then released onto the street.

No one was allowed to get near it, other than the Minstrels, as the so-called fun was supposed to be for them alone. The idea was that the Minstrels had to hold onto the slippery and dangerous bull long enough to cut off some of its hair. This task had to be done by sunset and the hair presented to prove that it had been achieved. When successful, the bull was captured with a rope and dragged to the bailiff's house and then to the bull ring in Tutbury High Street. Its misery was not yet over, as it was next baited three times with dogs. After the bait, the bull was presented to the 'King of Music'. It was then killed or sold to the bailiff who sent the animal to the Duke of Devonshire's estate at Hardwick. Here it was fattened up, despite its injuries, before being slaughtered at Christmas and given to the poor.

If the Minstrels were unsuccessful and the bull could not be knocked off the bridge before it escaped over the River Dove into the neighbouring county of Derbyshire, it belonged, in theory, to the Prior of Tutbury. However, in reality it became the property of the men of Derbyshire. Because of this, the event later deteriorated into a battle between the men of Staffordshire and Derbyshire. The Minstrels' rights were forgotten. The Derbyshire men tried to drive the bull into their county, whilst the Staffordshire men became hell-bent on preventing it. Both sides frequently attacked one another with cudgels and the event became a violent free-for-all fight. Finally, the people of Tutbury grew tired of the interference from Derbyshire and petitioned for the annual event to be halted. It was abolished in 1778 by the Duke of Devonshire.

The sport of bull-running was also popular in certain areas of London. Although it was initially held on Sundays, it achieved a larger following when held on Mondays. This was because men were at work in the city and many left their jobs and joined in the fun of the bull-run. By the end of the chase, several hundred men ran alongside or followed the animal, which was slaughtered when finally cornered. The East End of London became a favourite area to hold such events and Bethnal Green was one of the most popular. Despite the danger to passers-by in the streets, such pursuits were still taking place until the 1830s.

The normally accepted form of bull baiting was entirely different from bull-running. In a bull bait, the bull was always tethered and not allowed to run and usually a single dog at a time was unleashed to attack it. Bull baiting again became very popular in Elizabethan times, especially with the poorer classes. However, Queen Elizabeth I occasionally entertained visiting royalty, ambassadors and diplomats with the sport but the Royals in general much preferred the bear bait. Despite this preference, both King James I and King Charles I used a mixture of bull and bear baiting to amuse their guests.

King James tried to suppress bull baiting on Sundays, as he had done with bear baiting, but in any event he was not an enthusiastic follower of the former. The limited royal patronage declined after the death of Charles II in 1685, and Queen Anne when she ascended the throne in 1702 discouraged such activities. Bull baiting then became the sole prerogative of the working classes, and as with bear baiting the preferred day was a Sunday. Many people thought that the meat from a bull was always more tender after the animal had been baited. Certain bye-laws were passed in some areas stipulating this requirement, before the bull could be slaughtered for food. In the summer, the baiting and slaughtering of a bull in public reassured the purchasers of the meat that it was fresh. In the winter, the meat could be salted.

In a typical bull bait, a rope about fifteen feet long was tied around the base of the animal's horns, or to a fitted neck collar. The rope was then tied to an iron ring fixed to a sturdy stake, driven securely into the ground. The length of rope allowed the bull to turn around, when it wanted, within a circular area having an approximate diameter of thirty feet. As the nose of the bull was very sensitive, a small hole was sometimes dug in the ground to allow the bull to protect it, to a limited extent, during the bait. Often, a bull would paw a hole for itself, instinctively knowing that it would be rendered almost helpless if a dog seized its nose. The bulls selected for baiting were always massive and powerful.

The dogs were unleashed in turn and the early dogs used were large mastiffs. These proved unsuitable for the sport, as they were too cumbersome and slow and could not survive in the arena for long.

They were also too large to keep their heads and bodies low to avoid being impaled or tossed by the bull's horns. These early dogs were trained to go for the bull's belly and genitals but later special breeds were developed which went solely for the nose. These were cross-bred to produce a low-slung dog with a wide face and undershot jaw and eventually the true bulldog was developed, a dog endowed with great courage. The bulldog breed slowly died out after the banning of baiting but later breeders re-introduced it and the dog has now become a well-loved gentle household pet, the breeders having successfully bred out its former aggressive tendency.

The bulldogs when released in turn to bait a bull were trained to keep low and aim for the nose of the animal. If a dog successfully seized the bull by the nose, the accomplishment was described as 'pinning the bull'. Occasionally, a dog held on tenaciously to the nose without releasing its hold, even though the bull swung it around violently in the air to dislodge it. When a dog successfully achieved this holding feat, the process became known as 'pinning and holding the bull'. Sometimes the dog was even successful in bringing the bull down to the ground.

Eventually, the dog would be thrown off by the infuriated bull, often as high as twelve feet or more in the air. This tossing of the bull was called 'hyking' or 'hikeing'. The owners or handlers of the dogs would desperately try to break the fall of their own dog to save it breaking its neck, by catching it in a broad apron, or easing its lofty descent to the ground with their arms, arched backs or sometimes long staves. These men who actively participated in the sport were known as 'bull-hankers'. A dog was tossed high by the bull when it got its horns under the dog's belly. The bull did not normally gore the dog because if its horns were very sharp, they were encased in wooden sheaths. Often when the bull was weakened, the dogs would not be thrown off and they held on tenaciously with their clamped jaws. In this case, the only way to make the dog loosen its grip was for the handler to drag it off by the tail, or by forcing open its jaws with a lever. In extreme cases, the method was to blow flour into the dog's nostrils to block them, so it had to open its mouth to breathe.

Samuel Pepys in his diary described one visit he made with his wife, after dinner, to a baiting in London. He observed that one of the dogs was even tossed by the bull into one of the theatre boxes. However, Pepys was an infrequent visitor to the baiting arenas. He considered them 'a very rude and nasty pleasure and a strange sport for a gentleman'.

When a bull became cowed or too weak to fight, the enraged crowd would often give voice to their feelings and actively indulge in even greater depravity by tormenting the bull further to enliven it. Pepper was frequently blown into the animal's nostrils and, if this did not

Badger Baiting
(*H.B. Chalon*)

work, salt or other corrosive substances were rubbed into its wounds or hot water poured into its ears. This terrible cruelty could culminate with the cutting of the hooves of the bull to enrage it further.

In the established bull baiting arenas in the towns, substantial gambling took place on the outcome of the matches between owners' dogs. Sporting nobles were known to wager more than 100 guineas a time on individual contests. On a smaller scale, in the country areas, local people who followed the sport would risk five pennies or even a shilling a time to let their dog have a chance of 'pinning' the bull.

In a similar routine to bear baiting, the bull was often taken into the village or town by a travelling bullward, or bullard, who would attempt to gather a crowd together by first parading the animal through the streets. The procession was frequently led by a pipe player and the bull was decorated with flowers. The bull was often scarred and battered from previous encounters with dogs because good fighting bulls were not always slaughtered after a bait but kept to fight again. If a bull was not securely tethered to a stake, it sometimes broke free and pandemonium would reign. The crowd would scatter and several people might be injured by trampling or even killed. The bull would then be chased until it could be cornered and slaughtered. The meat was then sold to the local people.

The sport gained a huge following in the Midlands and especially in Birmingham, where there was a baiting arena until 1773. The famous area known as 'The Bull Ring', in the heart of present-day Birmingham's commercial and shopping centre, reminds us of its history. In London during the eighteenth and nineteenth centuries, a favourite place for bull baiting was at Tothill Fields, Millbank, which was one of the so-called rough areas close to the city. Often a baiting took place there, after the conclusion of a bare fist fight. Baiting became so popular that many etchings and prints were made of bull baiting scenes. People could also purchase pottery figures of bull and dog baits from the Staffordshire potteries, as ornaments to adorn the mantelpieces of their homes.

When the baiting of bulls was banned, it deprived thousands of working-class people throughout England of one of their favourite pastimes. Many turned their attention to dog fighting which had also been made illegal but was easier to stage in secret. It was often held at night to avoid police attention. The Black Country became the traditional stronghold of the sport. Earlier experience had shown that the bulldog, although excellent for the bait, was not quick enough to provide an effective and entertaining fight with another bulldog. However, cross-breeding with terriers produced an agile, intelligent dog with the additional advantage of the bulldog's courage and tenacity. The English white terrier and the black-and-tan terrier were both used to establish, with the English bulldog, a new breed known as the bull terrier, or the 'half-and-half' breed. It was also called the pit dog and eventually the Staffordshire bull terrier. This became the true fighting dog and one not only endowed with great courage, agility and ferocity but one seemingly unaffected by pain. Ironically, the Staffordshire bull terrier only gained official recognition as a distinct breed in 1835, the same year that dog baiting was officially banned in England.

Before the ban, the favourite day for dog fighting was a Sunday and in the early nineteenth century it was quite common to observe fifty or more bull terriers tied up outside a public house. Their owners would be inside drinking heavily whilst they arranged the matches between their dogs. Landlords often encouraged brutal sports, in order to entice customers in and to buy liquor. Eventually, magistrates started to refuse licences because of the public disturbances caused by the dog fights which took place later near the public houses.

As well as the general ban of 1835 on all forms of baiting, dog fighting was more strongly and specifically banned under a later Act of 1911. Despite this further law, fights between bull terriers were arranged surreptitiously until the 1930s. It is possible that they are still taking place, for the Royal Society for the Prevention of Cruelty to Animals prosecuted seven men as recently as 1985 for partici-

A Pugilist

pating in dog fighting.

As well as dog fighting, the rough sport of terrier rat catching had gained popularity in the nineteenth century. Betting often took place on the number of rats a terrier could kill in a given time. The rats were first caught by a rat-catcher and released in front of the terrier in a twelve-foot square pit at the beginning of each contest. It is possible that some of the rats were doped, on occasions, to achieve a high kill rate by a dog owner, especially when the gambling stakes were high. In the 1820s, a famous dog called 'Billy', or 'Billie' as he was sometimes known, set many records. Both the dog and its owner had lost an eye in their ratting exploits. Billy was reputed to have been able to kill fifty rats in a few minutes and this feat he repeated on several occasions. He claimed the astonishing record of once killing 100 rats in a little over six minutes, if this can be believed. Some reports suggest it took twelve minutes. When the courageous dog eventually died, it was taken to a taxidermist to be preserved and was later exhibited proudly on the bar of Tom Cribb's Union Arms in Panton Street, just off the Haymarket in London. Tom Cribb, the landlord, was the former great Regency pugilist, who took over the pub when he retired from fighting. The dog was further immortalized by the making of a well-known sporting print.

Generally, through the centuries, distinctions between country and urban baiting sports were not particularly apparent. Nevertheless, the baiting of badgers attracted many supporters in the country regions but a more limited number in the rougher areas, in and around the cities. For example, publicans at Smithfield in London encouraged badger baiting. However, the so-called sport never gained the large country-wide following achieved by bull baiting. It reached its height of popularity in the nineteenth century and took place at fairs and race courses.

The badger is one of our larger native wild mammals and, although baited, was never seriously hunted in England. In medieval times, a few were killed by the very poor to use the skin to make shoes for themselves. Later, the skin was fashioned to line coats and the bristles used for shaving brushes. In the distant past, badgers may have had enemies other than man. This theory may explain why they remain very wary and usually hidden from view in their underground homes, or setts, during the hours of daylight. They are mainly nocturnal creatures and can usually only be seen out at dusk or immediately before dawn.

This nocturnal habit made the task of the hunter easier in the past. He knew where the quarry would be during the hours of daylight, as the badger used the same sett year after year. The location of the setts would be well-known, as badgers love to make their subterranean homes by digging under well-drained banks, shaded by trees or bushes. Elders are always favoured as badgers love the berries. In the south of England, woods containing oak trees are much liked by the badger, especially when adjacent to pasture land. They also occasionally live in quarries and cliffs. The badger population was widespread in England during the seventeenth and eighteenth centuries but seriously declined in the nineteenth century owing to their persecution.

Badger setts consist of chambers and tunnels, between thirty and sixty feet long, and they have several entrances. A good indication of a badger sett is the pile of discarded straw bedding strewn nearby. When badgers were sought in their setts in the past, small dogs, such as terriers, were placed at the entrance holes to prevent escape, before digging commenced. Then the digger sent another terrier underground to locate the badger. He would often employ a listening rod to find the spot immediately above the growling and noise emanating from the dog and badger below. The end of the rod was sometimes fitted with an ear trumpet to amplify the sound. When the badger was dug out and exposed, it was seized around the neck by steel badger tongs, which were specifically made for the purpose, in the shape of callipers with long handles. The badger had to be handled carefully by the digger because it possessed a three-foot-long, strong barrel-shaped body with short powerful feet, each equipped with five menacing long claws, especially the front ones. The badger had strong jaws and sharp teeth as well. It was also extremely brave when attacked which was, of course, an essential characteristic of an animal for baiting purposes. The tongs assisted the digger to get the badger into a sturdy sack without being bitten. The sack was then secured at its neck by a buckle and strap. Eyelets pierced in the bag allowed the badger to breathe when inside the sack.

In the baiting spectacle, the badger was usually placed in a pit, or a hole dug in the ground. Its short blunt tail was fitted with a chain which was attached to a stake driven into the base of the pit. The badger was then baited with dogs, normally terriers or bull terriers. Wagering took place amongst the owners of the dogs but frequently up to half-a-dozen dogs could be killed by the badger, before its own tormented body succumbed and it died itself. In the event of the badger surviving the dogs, the brave creature was usually clubbed to death after the baiting. The venue for baiting was often the backyard of a public house. Sometimes, the badger's tail would be cruelly nailed to the ground and the added torment of the tail wound increased its suffering during the bait.

In another form of badger baiting, the badger was put into a wooden box with an open top covered with wire netting. The only way in or out of the box was through a tunnel made of wood, which was about ten feet long and attached to the box. A terrier of suitable size was sent up the tunnel to attack the badger. Both animals would try to clamp their jaws on one another and the terrier would attempt to drag the badger down the tunnel. As both animals were renowned for their bravery and tenacity, the fight could continue for a very long time. Again heavy wagering formed a part of the proceedings. The cruelty to the badger was sometimes made even more barbarous by the cutting of its lower jaw, to make the baiting contest more favourable to the dog. Yet another variation of badger baiting was to put the animal in a large barrel or cask placed sideways on the ground and to let a terrier try to drag it out. A wooden box without a long tunnel was also sometimes used. The participants bet on how many times a bull terrier could 'draw' the badger from its box in a set period of time. As soon as the badger was drawn out it was replaced in the box, so the horrendous procedure could be repeated by the same dog and the 'drawing' contest continued. Often it was difficult to separate the badger and the dog. The owner of the latter resorted to holding the dog by its leg in the air and biting its tail to make it release its hold on the badger.

Badger baiting had begun in earnest by the seventeenth century. It was legally banned by the general Act of 1835, but it was difficult to suppress unofficial baitings. Even as late as 1897, a prosecution took place at Preston in Lancashire for badger baiting. There must have been many more unrecorded cases. It was not until late in the twentieth century, in 1973, that badgers became legally and specifically protected against all forms of persecution. The Badgers Act of 1973 protected them more thoroughly than ever before. Unfortunately, the bovine tuberculosis outbreak in 1975 came almost immediately after the bill was enacted, so the killing of badgers in their setts by gassing was allowed, on licence from the Ministry of Agriculture. This was eventually banned in 1982; experience had shown that any badger which survived the gas could move to another sett and spread the disease. In addition, any other wild animal, such as the fox, which sometimes shared the badgers' sett was being accidentally killed by the gassing.

The original Badgers Act of 1973 was amended by the Wildlife and Countryside Act of 1981, together with a further amendment made in 1985. These reinforced the law on the unauthorized killing or capture of badgers. Despite the ban, a few incidents were reported of baiting taking place and this led to the formation of various badger protection groups. The Badger Protection Act of 1991, updated in 1992, gives powers to the judiciary to send convicted diggers and baiters to prison and also to disqualify them from owning dogs. The new law gives protection to the setts, as well as to the animal. It is therefore now illegal to tamper or interfere with a badger sett. This has implications for the fox-hunting community because if a fox, during the chase, goes to ground in a badger sett, a terrier can no longer be sent down to 'bolt' the fox for the hunt to continue.

The various local badger protection groups around the country now form part of The National Federation of Badger Groups. These groups not only protect the badgers and their setts but also monitor badger population. Their members enjoy the privilege of viewing these handsome mammals, with their white heads and black stripes over each ear and eye, when they leave their underground homes. The male badger, or boar, has a broader head and thicker neck than the female sow. The average weight of the male is about 25.5 lb (11.6 kg), whilst the female weighs about 23.5 lb (10.1 kg). Unfortunately, the only view the average member of the public has of the badger is by the roadside after the animal has been killed accidentally by a car. Man and the motor car are the sole enemies of the badger and many are killed during their nocturnal wanderings across our roads. In some areas of the country, special badger ways under roads and electrified railways have been constructed to allow the animals to travel more safely along their routes. However, it frequently proves difficult to make badgers use them initially and to accept them as part of their territory. Various enticements sometimes encourage them. For example, one man put badger scent on his coat and crawled through a new badger tunnel after it was constructed under the M5 motorway at Wellington, in Somerset.

When the animal baiting sports finally lost favour in the nineteenth century, the public's thirst for savagery and blood was quickly satisfied by paying more attention to brutal prizefights, arranged between bare fist, or bare knuckle, fighters. These had been in existence for many years before. Paradoxically, bare knuckle fighting was illegal throughout its entire history, although it often gained high-ranking approval. Many aristocrats took pride in hiring and sponsoring the fighters. They sometimes wagered huge sums, ranging from ten thousand to forty thousand guineas, on the result of an individual contest. These were often arranged to be fought on private land to escape the attention of the law. The majority took place in the south of England. One of the earliest recorded bare fist fights took place in January 1681 between a footman and a butcher. The contest was held to entertain the Duke of Albermarle. Although many brutal fights took place during the following decades, it was not until the early eighteenth century that the first resemblance of a type of prizefight championship was recognized. Jack Broughton, a famous fighter himself, laid down the first significant rules in 1743. These regulated prizefighting for well over a century, with only minor changes. It was much later, in the Regency period, that the greatest popularity for the pugilistic sport was reached and this only declined at the end of the nineteenth century. Prizefighting attracted huge audiences. For example, when Dutch Sam defeated Medley on 31st May 1810, over ten thousand people watched the fight. The contest lasted for forty-nine rounds and the prize was two hundred guineas.

Prizefighting became a favourite event at many country fairgrounds, as well as the more established venues in the cities. Later, the boxers wore very thin skin gloves instead of using their bare fists. The familiar padded gloves of today were not introduced until 1867, and the Marquess of Queensbury gave his name and patronage to the new rules when they were first used in 1892. However, it was a slow process before gloves finally replaced bare fists in 1895.

Fighting-cock in Full Feather (*J.F. Herring, Sen.*)

2   Cock-fighting

The sport of cock-fighting was established in very ancient times throughout many Eastern countries, such as China, India and Persia. It spread slowly westwards and possibly reached Greece in about 500 BC. One story relates that Themistocles observed two cocks fighting when he was leading his men into battle against the Persians. He praised the tenacity and obstinacy of the cocks in battle and thus raised the morale and courage of his own troops. The Athenians defeated the Persians and the date of the victory was celebrated by an annual cock-fight. The fighting cocks were probably imported into Greece.

Cock-fighting met resistance in Italy initially but became popular there in about AD 100. The Romans then spread cock-fighting through Europe and eventually participated in the sport in England. However, the history of the exact origin of the fighting gamecock in England remains obscure. It is not clear whether the Romans imported them, or if they were perhaps already native birds. It is possible that domesticated fowls had previously been introduced to Britain for the table and perhaps even for cock-fighting. Some may have been obtained from Germany. Whatever the origin of the cocks, it is known that the Romans praised them highly and even buried their favourite birds with great ceremony, in special urns. Eventually, the birds became known as the Old English gamecock.

Cock-fighting held its popularity from the twelfth to the early nineteenth century, and in its heyday, in Georgian and Regency times, it entertained thousands of people from Kings to commoners. In fact, it became the most popular sport in England. The season for cock-fighting was nearly all the year round, except for the months of June and July. Sundays and church festivals became favourite occasions for the sport. It was always suspended in times of plague, together with most other sporting activities. As with all blood sports, Henry VIII was a keen supporter and the Stuarts, such as James I and Charles II, also became extremely enthusiastic. James I was reputed to watch cock-fighting twice a week. The rules and orders for 'cocking', as it was called, were established in the reign of Charles II.

Henry VIII in the 1530s ordered his own Royal Cockpit to be built near the Palace of Westminster. It was constructed at the edge of St James's Park, or in 'St James's Fields', as the area was known at that time, close to Birdcage Walk at Whitehall. The Royal Cockpit was an enclosed indoor pit, like most of the later ones built in London, and it was in the form of a wooden amphitheatre. Henry appointed his own

King's Cock-master to preside over the royal pit, or the Cock-in-Court as it became known. Here were staged many cock-fights over the years, although it was converted into a playhouse in about 1604. It was then built with stone walls and fitted with a conical roof of steep pitch, with a lantern above. The building was about fifty feet in diameter. It ceased to be used as a theatre after 1664 and in 1697 was again altered to be used as a Privy Council Room. In the reign of Charles II, additional royal cockpits were built outside London. These included The Royal Cockpit at Windsor and His Majesty's Cockpit at Newmarket.

Other famous London cockpits in addition to the Whitehall pit were situated in Jewin Street, off Aldergate Street near the Barbican, Jermyn Street, Drury Lane and Clerkenwell, where the New Red Lion Cockpit was built. The pit at Drury Lane was constructed in 1609. It was named the Cockpit Theatre but it was relatively small, being only fifty feet square. During 1616, it was tiered and a roof was installed over it so that plays could be held there as well. Its name was changed in 1617, in James I's reign, to the Phoenix Theatre, after the cockpit building had been burned down on Shrove Tuesday of that year by rioting apprentices. The new roofed theatre built in its place housed a mixture of stage plays and cock-fights. The Phoenix Theatre was later demolished in 1649. Before permanent theatres were built, actors staged their plays in the courtyards of inns, the galleries around the yard providing the space for the audience.

Most of the very early cockpits were built outdoors in the form of circular hollows in the ground. These were often surrounded by low banks and ditches. Seats for the spectators were cut in the earthen banks around the pits. The cocks were allowed quite a large area to fight in, as some of the outdoor pits were up to a hundred feet in diameter. Smaller versions of the large outdoor cockpits later became popular in the backyards of taverns and fights were also held in village churchyards. Some of the outdoor pits were roofed with tiles or thatch, to give some shelter to the cocks and the ring of spectators who surrounded them. These pits resembled the circular bandstands we have in our parks today. In the seventeenth century, the sport started to cater for a more sophisticated clientele and small pits, under complete cover, were built indoors. Eventually, nearly every town in England and Wales possessed a cockpit, although they were not introduced into Scotland until 1681. In addition to the permanent cockpits, many make-shift ones were also available at such places as fairgrounds, markets and race courses.

'Cocking' became popular even in schools, especially on Shrove Tuesday, when other sports such as pancake races also traditionally took place. London schoolboys, even as early as the twelfth century in

Henry II's reign, were encouraged to bring cocks to school when they arrived in the morning, so that the master had plenty of time to arrange the fights throughout the day. The boys purchased their cocks with money given to them by their parents and this money became known as cockpence. The schoolmaster had the incentive to organize the fights, as he kept any birds killed, as a reward for his efforts. He may also originally have been the supplier of the birds for the cock-fights. For variety, the master sometimes tethered the birds at a fixed distance away from his pupils, so that the boys could use them as targets while they threw stones at them. Sticks were also used as missiles and this variation became known as cock-throwing (this is described in more detail later). Cock-fighting at schools on Shrove Tuesday continued well into the eighteenth century, and not only in the city. For example, schoolboys at Wimborne Grammar School in Dorset still brought their fighting cocks to school. The master officiated over a draw to match the cocks and the fights continued all day until only one bird survived.

All the established indoor cockpits were circular and had a diameter of between twelve and twenty feet. Many were in the form of a stage raised about eighteen inches above the ground. The stage was surrounded by a barrier, which was less than two feet high to prevent the birds from falling off but at the same time did not interfere with the spectators' view. Those in the first row would often lean on the barrier, although they were not allowed to touch the cocks. The sides of the pit, or barrier, were made of wood and were often padded with chopped straw or hay and then covered with canvas. The floor of the pit was often covered with matting or carpet. Sometimes the floor was laid like a lawn with green turves instead and the use of these gave the nickname of 'The Sod' to the sport of cock-fighting.

In the early days of cock-fighting, the cocks fought one another to a finish, or to an agreed time limit set by the owners. Later, rules were introduced to allow the handler to withdraw his owner's bird at any time. A complete match, or battle, between gamecocks was known as a 'main' and there were many variations. The popular 'main' was an agreed odd number of fights arranged between different pairs of birds belonging to two owners, or 'cockers' as they were known. The odd number of battles ensured that there would always be a winner who was, of course, the owner, or cocker, who had the majority of victories with his team of birds. The favourite odd number of fights was seven.

Sometimes a time limit was set for the complete series of individual contests; for example, a long-main was a battle which could last over a period of four days or more. Alternatively, a short-main was not allowed to exceed three days. The individual fights between two cocks in a series could last up to an hour but sometimes they were over in just a few minutes.

Fighting-cock Trimmed (*J.F. Herring, Sen.*)

A Welsh-main was a knockout competition between sixteen to thirty-two pairs of birds, although sixteen was the more usual. After each individual battle, the victorious gamecock was re-matched with the winner from another fight. This elimination contest, by re-matching, continued until only one pair was left. The victor in this final battle became the overall winner of the Welsh-main. The most cruel of the many variations of cock-fights was the 'battle royal', which was particularly condemned by the moralists and also angered many other people. In this type of bloody main, a number of cocks were thrown into the cockpit to fight one another at the same time, until only one survived. The general depravity of cock-fighting was depicted by Hogarth in about 1750 in his picture, 'The Cockpit Royal'. He attempted to show how it brutalized men.

In a main, the birds were originally matched by their comparable size measurements but later the weights of the birds were used to ensure a fairer fight. It was realized that this was the vital factor and the earlier rules laid down by Charles II were changed. For battle-cocks, the weight normally varied between 3 lb 6 oz and 4 lb 8 oz.

A Contrasting Breed of Fighting-cock Trimmed (*H.G. Arnold*)

Cocks were transported to and from the cockpits in individual bags. When they had to be transported around the country, they travelled in special horse-drawn gamecock caravans. The sight of these caravans on the roads enraged many moralists.

Before the seventeenth century, cocks fought only with their beaks and natural spurs, the curved horn-shaped projections on the birds' legs. Owners often sharpened the beak and also the cock's spurs with a knife, although these were already lethal enough in a fight. During the seventeenth century, the richer owners started to fit artificial spurs to the cock's legs. The cock when 'heeled' with these was ready for the fight and when it stood with its legs close together the stance was called 'close-heeled'. This suggested the cock would probably be a powerful striker with its spurs, the reverse being the case if it stood with its legs wide apart.

The artificial spurs were slipped and securely fastened over the natural ones which would have been sawn off to form a stub. The artificial spurs were made of bone or metal. The latter became more common and were of steel, iron or silver. Different-length spurs were used: 'long-heels' were between 2 and 2½ inches long, whilst 'short-heels' were 1½ inches long. The shapes of the spurs also varied but the most common was the simple spur in the form of a curved stout needle. Other shapes were the 'sickle', 'lance' and 'penknife' spurs. The very rich owners always indulged in silver spurs, which were hallmarked and made by an expert silversmith. London became the centre for the craft and Cockspur Street acquired its name from the industry.

Before a battle and during training, the cock's feathers were trimmed. The neck feathers were clipped from head to shoulders and the wings shaped at the slope to a point. The comb was cut as short as possible to reduce the target area when pitted against an opponent. The rump feathers and hackle or neck feathers were also shortened. The birds were usually between one and two years old when submitted to their first battle. Normally, before a fight, the handler, 'pitcher' or 'setter-to' of the cock released the bird onto the pit floor, where it strutted around before being gathered up. The opposing handler then went through the same procedure before catching up his bird. There was then a short delay while any bets were struck amongst the spectators. The birds were then released at opposite sides of the pit at set 'scratch' marks and they immediately rushed at one another and the fight commenced. Often, the contest ended with the death of one of the cocks.

The fighting-cocks were by nature very game and courageous and a cock usually carried on the battle even after being blinded by a peck, a very frequent occurrence. Most contests were fought with intense fury, the cocks using both beaks and spurs for the attack. The very aggressive nature of the cock is perhaps more easily understood by considering the inherent pecking tendency of the fowl species. All domestic fowls were developed mainly from the Jungle fowl, *Gullus gallus*, and even present-day farm birds establish a relative rank order or hierarchy with the other birds in their group. The most aggressive bird, which pecks the others the most, becomes dominant and always has the first peck at the food. The second strongest pecker has the second choice of the food, and so on down the rank. A bird will never peck one higher in the social order but will peck at all the others below it. Generally, the male achieves the leadership of a group, as normally it is the most aggressive pecker. Two cocks placed together therefore ensures a bitter conflict.

At all cock-fights, appointed judges were in charge. The 'cockers' or 'pitters' normally selected one of the judges and he then chose another. Sometimes only one judge would officiate. No objections could be lodged against the judges' decisions, after any initial appeal had been considered and their verdict given. This was the theory but in practice many arguments ensued. After delivery of the cocks to the pit area, the 'cockers' were not allowed to touch the birds without obtaining official permission. Also, during the actual fight the 'pitters' were strictly forbidden to assist or touch the cocks in any way. In the unlikely event of two cocks not wanting to fight after being 'pitted', a count of a hundred was usually allowed before a new bird was introduced. The owners would then toss between themselves to decide which two of the three birds would fight. The judges declared a draw if the two selected birds would not do battle either.

In the unusual event of a gamecock deciding during a fight that it had had enough, it would sometimes indicate its intention by raising its hackles. The underside of a cock's hackle is edged with white feathers and displaying these led to the commonly used expression for cowardice of 'showing the white feather'. Many other familiar sayings owe their origins to the cockpit; terms such as 'showing a clean pair of heels' and 'pit against' are further examples. Many words now accepted in our everyday language come from the proud and domineering nature of the gamecock; words such as 'cocky', 'cocksure', 'cock-a-hoop' and 'cock-of-the-walk'. The word 'cockpit' itself was later used to denote an enclosed space, such as the cockpit of an aircraft.

If a cock became injured or badly distressed in any way during a contest, the proceedings would sometimes be halted by the judges. The pitters would then place the two birds to face one another, beak to beak. If the disabled cock did not strike out at the other, then the latter was declared the winner. All bets would then be settled and, as is usual in most forms of wagering, the bets could only be called off if both parties agreed to do so.

The size of bets laid varied enormously, from hundreds of guineas at

Cock-fighting. Set To
(*Henry Alken, Sen.*)

one end of the social scale in the city, to a prize of a farm animal, such
as a pig, in the poorer country regions. Nobles might wager a
hundred guineas on a single match but often the prize was much
inflated by the added stakes of five hundred guineas or more for the
winner of the complete main. One of the biggest betting mains was
between the Earl of Derby and Joseph Gilliver from Polesworth in
Warwickshire, both famous breeders of gamecocks. This took place at
Lincoln in 1830 and seven birds were entered from each side. The
individual wagers made were one thousand guineas on each match
and the added stake was five thousand guineas for the whole main.
These were huge sums when scaled up to present-day values. Joseph
Gilliver won the contest by five matches to two. The gambling was
not always just confined to the result of a fight. Bets were frequently
struck during the course of a contest, as the odds against the
opposing cocks constantly fluctuated.

The newspapers advertised the cock-fighting fixtures that were to
take place around the country, just as is done nowadays for racing,
football and cricket. Coal-mining areas became favourite places to
stage fights because of their large following of the sport. This was
despite high admission charges, and Newcastle boasted at least
seven cockpits around 1800. The Potteries also drew large crowds for

cock-fights. Many venues established annual dates and cock-fights were often held over a period of three days, a similar period to the more civilised county cricket matches. The 'Rules for Matching and Fighting Cocks' were published regularly in the *Racing Calendar*, together with the results of important mains. Newspapers carried all the names of the gamecocks that were declared to fight each day in the various mains, and even issued estimated prices for those interested in gambling on them. This bears a resemblance to the present-day practice of the publication of horse-racing fixtures and probable starting price odds in our newspapers.

Cock-fighting had other indirect links with horse racing in the fact that fights were often held at race courses, either before or after the meeting. The public frequently staked more money on the cock-fights than on the racing but this gradually changed when Charles II

Cock-fighting. Sparring (*Samuel Alken*)

started to patronize Newmarket in the seventeenth century and Arab blood was introduced to produce a better class of race horses. Later, at the beginning of the nineteenth century, Chester race week was the venue for some famous mains, and birds were entered by celebrated breeders, such as the locally famous Doctor Bellyse of Audlem in Cheshire.

The breeding of gamecocks was treated very seriously both by the humbler villager at a local rural level and by the more prosperous who attempted scientific and logical methods. For example, the superstitious rural breeder placed game-fowls' eggs in a convenient magpie's nest to be hatched. He thought that the chicks would prove to be much fiercer, having been hatched with the assistance of the magpie. The magpie was thought by many to be the protégé of the Devil or Evil One. This hopeful method, of course, completely ignored the breeding of the parent bird who created the eggs; it was based purely on local folklore.

The more scientific breeder relied mainly on pedigree selection and the crossing of strains from the most successful fighting birds developed over many years. This method could not guarantee success

Cock-fighting. Into Action (*Henry Alken, Sen.*)

Cock-fighting. Knock Down (*Hilton Pratt*)

but the odds were more favourable. In the seventeenth century, many of the fighting-cocks were bred in Norfolk. One of the largest breeders in England in the eighteenth century and early nineteenth century was the twelfth Earl of Derby. He was assisted by his chief man and 'cocker', a gentleman named Potter, and the Earl built and operated a very lavish cockpit at Preston. At one stage, the Earl of Derby was reputed to have housed three thousand gamecocks on his estate in a single year. On several occasions he bred over two thousand cocks a year and his keenness for the sport was obviously more important to him than the small fortune it cost him to pursue his hobby.

Lord Derby gave his name to some of the strains of cocks he bred for fighting to illustrate his ownership; for example, the Derby Black Red indicated both the owner and the breed of cock. A Black Red meant that the bird had a black breast but its hackle and saddle (the part of the back nearest to the tail) were red. As well as Black Reds, there was a host of other famous breeds of fighting-cocks, developed not only by Lord Derby but by the two other notable breeders of the day, Joseph Gilliver and Doctor Bellyse. There were other breeders as well. The names of the most illustrious breeds at the time were Blue Reds, Shropshire Reds, Taverner's Grays, Wednesbury Grays, Duckwings, White Game, Spangled Game, Pirchin Ducks, Pollcats, Gingers and various Piles (or Pyles). Doctor Bellyse favoured the White Piles and Cheshire Piles. Joseph Gilliver used several breeds and supplied many cocks to both George III and George IV. These cocks fought in the Westminster Cockpit. Many of the nobility indulged in cock-fighting and the Duke of Rutland in particular was a great supporter and patron of the sport.

From an early age, cocks were trained to become extremely fit by a controlled feeding and exercise regime. This was intensified about six weeks before a fight to increase stamina. The person who trained the cocks was in fact not known as a trainer but was always referred to as the individual who 'fed' the cocks for fighting. Many special diets

A Cock-fighting Scene
(*Henry Alken, Sen.*)

were formulated by the feeder and each individual favoured his own special recipe. Only the very best food was given to the cocks and this led to the expression 'to feed like a fighting cock'. Also, the finest-quality drinking water available was given to the birds. The cocks were not only exercised to reach peak condition but most also enjoyed massage treatment to tone their skin and muscles. After a fight, the wounds would be carefully dressed and the bird nursed back to health. During training, the birds' spurs were always heavily padded, with sheaths of leather called 'hots', when pitted against other cocks for practice fights. This was to ensure that the risk of injury in training was minimized, as the best birds were highly valued.

Many attempts were made through the centuries to abolish cock-fighting in England. These efforts were not usually on behalf of the cocks but were more to stifle some of the side-effects on the people who attended such contests, especially the heavy gambling associated with the sport. One of the very earliest attempts was made as long ago as 1366 in the reign of Edward III. The next attempt was by a proclamation issued in London in 1409. This banned anyone from levying money on a cock-fight, under the threat of imprisonment or a fine. Few appeared to take much notice of the order and wagering still continued quite openly. It was not until the strong Puritan protest, in the seventeenth century, that pressure was substantially increased to discourage the working class from gambling on such spectacles. Cock-fighting was prohibited by law in 1654 but again the public enthusiasm for the sport overcame this and it started to flourish again. Many paintings were done of cock-fights in the eighteenth and nineteenth centuries and a host of poems were written praising the great courage of the gamecock.

The general legal ban of 1835 to stop the baiting of animals did not immediately halt cock-fighting. In the same year, William IV had to prohibit cock-fighting in London by banning it within a five-mile radius of Temple Bar. The Society for the Prevention of Cruelty to Animals initiated at least twelve prosecutions for non-compliance with the 1835 Act between 1838 and 1841. In fact, one of the Society's inspectors was killed in a brawl when trying to stop a cock-fight in 1839. Further prosecutions were brought on many occasions between 1841 and 1849. It was not until 1849 that cock-fighting was specifically outlawed in a new Act and it was made illegal for a public cockpit to be used anywhere in the country. However, the fine for staging a cock-fight was only five pounds and as the profit from organizing a contest was well in excess of this, many carried on the sport in secret, especially in remote rural locations.

A few people were more bold and even arranged fights in public places. For example, in 1875 police broke up a cock-fight which was taking place on Aintree racecourse. Liverpool appears to have staged several illicit fights, as four men had earlier been prosecuted in the city in 1871. Even the Marquis of Hastings was prosecuted in 1863 for allowing a cock-fight to take place at his ancestral home, Donnington Hall. The mining communities also continued to stage many cock-fights and they remained very popular events in Northumberland until well into the 1870s. Strangely, the most unlikely places to find illegal cock-fights were the public houses, as the landlords were no longer willing to risk losing their licence, which was granted to them by the authorities.

It is known that cock-fights were still taking place in the Lake District during the 1930s and no doubt in many other locations as well. Even in England in the 1990s, the RSPCA Special Operations Unit still tries to track down and investigate any alleged clandestine cock-fights that are reported to them. Cock-fighting remains widespread in several parts of the world, especially in Asia and some South American countries, such as Haiti, Mexico and especially Puerto Rico, where it has always been an important sport.

The alternative sport of cock-throwing had a relatively small following in comparison with cock-fighting. It gained popularity in the Middle Ages and still continued (illegally) well into the nineteenth century. It was staged in any open space or field, in village churchyards, in school playgrounds and in the streets; the favourite occasions for the sport were public holidays, especially Shrove Tuesdays. The basic idea of the game was to throw a stick at a tethered live cock and knock it over. Relatively little gambling took place; the reward to the contestant was to keep the bird. The owner of the cock made a profit by charging the competitors a fee.

The cock, when young, underwent a training programme before it was submitted to a cock-shy competition. It was tethered to a peg driven into the ground by a short cord tied to one of its legs. The cock was taught to dodge sticks hurled at it. During training only very light sticks would be thrown to increase its nimbleness but without trying to injure the bird. A well-trained cock became quite expert at dodging missiles and its cleverness and agility could make a profit for the owner in later shying contests. However, it was rare for a cock to survive many contests and eventually it would be hit and claimed.

In competition, the cock was again tethered by the leg but this time much heavier wooden sticks were used as missiles. These were often broomsticks or similar objects. The competitors stood between twenty and thirty yards away from the cock but the favoured distance was often twenty-two yards, the same length as a cricket pitch. The competitors paid a fee of between one and three pennies to have a 'cock-shy'. This allowed them a set number of tries, usually three, to knock the cock over. Each contestant took turns at the shy.

If a competitor was successful, he was then allowed to rush forward and try to pick up the cock before it regained its feet. If achieving this, the contestant kept the cock but on failing to reach the bird in time, the cock remained the property of the owner.

As early as the eighteenth century many people, in addition to the Methodists, favoured the suppression of cock-throwing. They considered it to be unfair and extremely cruel, although many still tolerated cock-fighting. This was because the bird in cock-throwing had no real chance of escape, whilst in cock-fighting each cock had an equal chance of winning. This was the first glimmer of the sporting instinct which allows a quarry a chance of survival.

When cock-throwing contests became widely held in town streets, the sport achieved a reputation of being a nuisance and also a danger to passers-by. In view of this, many towns attempted to ban it; for example, the officials of Newbury in 1759 tried to prohibit cock-throwing in all their thoroughfares. However, the ban was difficult to enforce.

A variation of cock-throwing took place in some areas, such as North Walsham in Norfolk. This was conducted in the street by placing a cock in an earthenware pot, which had been specially made so that both the cock's head and tail would be seen. The pot containing the cock was suspended about thirteen feet above the street and people were invited to take a shy at it. The charge was about two pennies for four throws; if the pot was smashed and the bird released, the thrower kept the cock as his reward.

After 1835, the sport of cock-throwing was officially prohibited in all places throughout England. However, it still continued to a limited extent and an incident was reported of it at Quainton in Buckinghamshire in 1844. Even as late as the mid-1880s, a cock-throwing contest was held at Wakefield in Yorkshire and a number of people were prosecuted. In addition to the 1835 legislation, the Metropolitan Police Act 1839 and the Town Police Clauses Act 1847, both under criminal law, imposed penalties for keeping a place for baiting animals and this included cock-throwing and cock-fighting. The Protection of Animals Act 1911 gave further protection; it was applicable to domestic fowls as well as to animals. More recently, the Cock-Fighting Act 1952 made it an offence to be in possession of any instrument or appliance which could be used in the fighting of domestic fowls.

Peregrine Falcon with
Dead Woodcock
(*J. Giles*)

3   Falconry (Hawking)

The true origin of the art of falconry fades into the mists of time. In essence, the sport consists of the training of hawks to take wild prey in its natural habitat but not to retrieve it. Historians suggest that it was possibly practised in China as far back as 2000 BC. It had probably spread throughout Asia by about 800 BC but this is not certain. There is more solid evidence that it was practised in Japan around AD 250 using birds imported from China. It became well established in Japan during the following century. However, falconry appears to have arrived much later in England. The earliest records suggest AD 600 but the sport did not make rapid progress until it was more widely introduced by French noblemen in about AD 860. The Saxon kings, Alfred the Great and Athelstan in the tenth century, and Edward the Confessor and King Harold in the following century, were all keen falconers. King Harold appears in the Bayeux Tapestry with two hounds by his side and a hawk perched on his fist. This type of tapestry, depicting hunting scenes, later became a favourite subject of many medieval artists.

The Normans swiftly made laws to ensure that only persons of the highest rank were allowed to keep hawks. The penalties for illegal hawking were harsh. William the Conqueror brought over with him from France his own entourage of falconers, all dressed in smart livery. This tradition of formal dress was continued throughout the following centuries by all the kings, when they appointed their Royal Falconers. They were always expensively dressed and most of those selected for the post were landed gentry, as the post held high esteem. Many kings received hawks as gifts from visiting nobility and the official presentation of the bird was always made with great ceremony. The king would accept the hawk on a beautiful richly gold-embroidered hawking glove, although hardly the ideal material to withstand the sharp talons of the bird. The use of this glove was probably restricted solely to the ceremonial process and never worn for hunting.

In the early days of hawking, the prime objective was to capture birds or small mammals for food. The nobles sought herons as the most prestigious quarry, to serve at their large medieval banquets. Herons, or cranes as they were also called, often formed the centre-piece of a lavish meal. Long-winged peregrine falcons were normally used in pairs, or a cast, to hunt the heron, which often proved a most elusive quarry. The attack of two falcons, alternating their 'stoops' or high dives, prevented the heron from climbing too high, or flying too far away from the falconer. The ownership of a cast of peregrine falcons became a very important status symbol. Heron colonies were established at traditional nesting sites and one of the oldest known ones was at Chilham, in Kent, dating back to 1293. A heronry was often named after the village, farm, hill or house which was the closest to it. For example, the origin of the word Herne Hill, near London, comes from the hill with the heronry on the top of it.

The importance of falconry to obtain food became widely recognized, although it had been a well-established method of taking wildfowl before the thirteenth century. Henry VIII later started the whole concept of the granting of Royal Warrants – that is, 'by appointment' – by bestowing his coveted coat-of-arms crest on a Mr Thomas Hewytt. This warrant was 'to serve the Court with Swannes and Cranes and all Kinds of Wildfoule'. Many of these would have been caught by falconry. Although originally only nobles were allowed to own hawks, when the Carta de Foresta was obtained from Henry III in 1225, all freemen became eligible. The Carta de Foresta therefore reduced the game rights of the nobility. It also abolished the severe penalties of death and mutilation for offences against the Forest Laws. Most freemen, however, could not afford the peregrine falcon but instead used the short-winged goshawk to hunt for their quarry. This became known as the 'cook's bird', as it successfully took a huge variety of game and provided a good supply of food for the human diet.

Although the general term 'hawks' is frequently used to describe both falcons and hawks, they are in fact different. The long-winged falcons (*Falconidae*) are birds such as the peregrine, whilst the hawks are short-winged birds (*Accipitridae*), such as the goshawk. In a similar manner, while the general term 'falconer' is often used to describe a person who handles both falcons and hawks, the definition is not strictly correct. In fact, a falconer trains and flies falcons but the person who trains and flies short-wing hawks is properly called an 'austringer'. The female peregrine is about a third larger in size than the male (called a tiercel) and the female is properly considered to be the supreme falcon. The merlin, although smaller than the peregrine, is another bird classified as a falcon and it is Britain's smallest falcon. Falcons require large open areas in which to operate. As well as long pointed wings, the birds have broad shoulders and dark eyes. Falcons are the most majestic of birds and can swoop with great speed and accuracy onto their quarry.

The short-winged hawks, such as the goshawk, buzzard and sparrowhawk, usually have golden or yellow eyes and long tails. They can hunt over much smaller areas than the falcon. Although freemen could own hawks, a social strata still existed in medieval times as to the particular type of bird. For example, king and nobles greatly valued the female peregrine falcon, which they hunted with from their gloved fist, both on horseback and from the ground. The merlin became the favourite of the ladies because it is smaller but it could still successfully take small birds and partridges. Lower down the social scale, the yeomen used the goshawk, whilst the sparrowhawk became the accepted bird for the clergy and also some of the ladies. The peasants had to be content with the more humble kestrel.

Until the twentieth century, hawks were traditionally taken from the wild to train for falconry. This was done generally in three different ways. The first was to take a young hawk from the nest when it was fully feathered but as yet still flightless; this type was known as the 'eyas'. The second method was to catch a one-year-old bird using a net. These immature birds were known as 'passagers' because they were often taken when they were migrating. The third way was to capture a fully mature adult bird, called a 'haggard'. Experience showed that although the haggard was already an extremely skilled and efficient hunter in the wild, it had the disadvantage of being difficult to tame. The reverse was true for the young birds; they had to be taught the lengthy procedure of hunting but had the advantage of relative ease of taming and getting accustomed to the falconer handling them. The peregrine falcon was the easiest to tame and train.

The basic training of a hawk to hunt at the command of man has changed little during the history of falconry. It has always demanded knowledge and a detailed understanding of the habits of the bird. The art also requires great patience and the achieving of trust between the hawk and the falconer. It is impossible to punish a hawk, as any hint of anger would not only upset the bird but render it entirely unsuitable for falconry. The gaining of confidence takes a great deal of time and effort. The training has always revolved around food provision to the bird and getting it to tolerate stroking and handling by the falconer. The food must always be fresh and natural to the hawk. In the early stages, the falconer carries the hawk on his fist for several hours each day.

The birds appear to offer no objection to hoods being put over their heads, as it has a calming effect and prevents them becoming alarmed at sudden movements. The concept of the hood was brought to England by men returning from the Crusades; before this time its use was unknown. The hoods designed for use by the English kings

A Hobby Hawk and Prey (*Robert Wilkinson Padley*)

were usually made of soft leather, or velvet, which had been beautifully enriched with fine needlework. Tufts of coloured feathers were added to the top of the hood to decorate it further. The tuft also had a practical use as it allowed the hood to be removed quickly to let the bird sight its quarry. Most hoods for general use were made of soft leather and were more simply decorated by topping them with a simple plume of feathers. There are now two main types of hood, known as the European (or Dutch) and the Indian. It is thought that the former type developed from the original designs brought back by the Crusaders. One main difference between the European and the Indian hood is that the former fits the bird's head more comfortably, as it is a heavier construction and less likely to be thrown off by the

Hawk on Gloved Fist

bird. Another major difference is that the European hood has a much smaller opening for the hawk's beak than the Indian hood.

In earlier times, when hawks were trapped in the wild, a hood called a 'rufter' was placed on the bird's head immediately after capture to calm it. This was a simple general-purpose hood which was only used as a temporary measure to calm the bird until the hawk could be fitted later with a better hood. A plume of feathers was never used on a 'rufter' hood as it was not required to be decorative and the absence of such an addition made it more difficult for the hawk to discard it. Hoods appear to 'hoodwink', or trick, the bird into thinking that daytime is night-time, with the result that the bird becomes quiet and peaceful.

After the hawk has become tame and content to feed from the fist, the hood is removed so that the bird can become accustomed to the sight and noise of people, dogs and other distractions. The process takes a considerable time and eventually the hawk is taught to fly to the falconer's fist. As well as assisting in training, hoods are also used when birds are being transported, but it depends on their individual temperament. In the hunting field, hoods are mainly used on the larger long-winged falcons until they are sent after their quarry. However, they are not always needed.

The use of hoods in training has superseded the commonly used seventeenth-century method of 'seeling', an operation carried out upon the capture of a wild hawk to help it recover from the shock and assist early training. 'Seeling' involved sewing together the eyelids temporarily to blindfold the bird and it is still done in many Middle Eastern countries. In medieval times, merchants also performed 'seeling' on their hawks to calm them during their journey to England by ship. In the seventeenth century, the barbaric procedure was to pass a needle, threaded with a fine linen or silk thread, through the lower eyelid of the hawk. Only one small neat stitch was necessary. The thread was then passed over the crown of the bird's head and stitched to the lower eyelid of the other eye. Again only one stitch was needed. The thread was then gently tightened by twisting it together and tying at the back and this had the effect of slowly pulling up the lower eyelids over the falcon's eyes until they were nearly closed.

As the bird became calm the thread was slightly loosened. Without having been 'seeled', the bird would have been greatly alarmed by the bright light of day after capture from the wild. The loosening process was done gradually and each day the eyes were allowed to open a little more by untwisting the thread. Eventually the eyes were fully opened and the thread removed. Instead of sewing a stitch in the lower eyelids, sometimes the stitching was carried out through the upper eyelids and in this case the thread would have been tied under the hawk's curved beak. After the removal of the stitches, a leather hood was placed over the bird's head when it was resting in the mews. This helped it to remain peaceful. Later it was taken onto the falconer's fist for training and eventually for hunting.

Light short leather straps, called 'jesses', are always fitted to both legs of the hawk and these remain on the bird at all times. The straps are kept as short as practical to prevent them becoming entangled or caught on the branch of a tree when the bird flies. These jesses help the falconer to restrain the hawk when it is perched on the gloved fist. Normally, a falconer carries the bird on his left hand, so only this one glove is necessary. A sturdy glove is essential to resist the rough grip of the sharp talons, and thick genuine buckskin is accepted as the best material for a falconer's glove, although other types of leather are often used with small falcons and hawks owing to the difficulty in obtaining real buckskin.

Special tiny, light bells are also attached to the legs of the falcons and in the case of short-winged hawks, sometimes to the tails. The bells are secured to the legs, just above the jesses, by short leather strips known as 'bewits'. The bells enable the falconer to hear and then locate the hawk when it has disappeared into a bush or wood, after killing its quarry under cover of shielding undergrowth. The bells are made in different sizes to accommodate different-sized birds. Small hawks usually carry one bell only but larger ones may be fitted with two, one to each leg. When two bells are used, some falconers suggest that one bell should be a different note to the other, so that the sound can be more readily heard.

In the fourteenth and fifteenth centuries, Milan was an established manufacturing centre. The Italians became renowned for the excellent quality and craftsmanship of the hawks' bells which were exported to many countries around the world. Today, the most highly prized hawks' bells are made in Amritsar and Lahore in Pakistan. The technical reason for the high quality of these bells remains somewhat obscure. Spectrographic metallurgical analysis shows that the metal used possesses a host of impurities and some suggest that these allow the bell to give a clearer note than when a purer metal is used. The non-symmetrical shaped clapper in the bell means that it produces a ring at the slightest movement of the bird. In general, thin metal bells yield the loudest sound but the thinner the metal the shorter the life of the bell. Nowadays, bells are also manufactured in both Europe and America.

In addition to helping the falconer to find his hawk when free, the use of hawk bells gives warning if the bird flies off the perch too often or is uncomfortable when resting in the mews. A leash, traditionally consisting of a long thong of leather, is normally fitted to a hawk in the mews to allow it to fly a little from its perch. One end of the leash is tied to the perch whilst the other is attached, via a swivel, to the

Falconer with Hawk-
ing Dogs (*Richard
Ansdell*)

joined jesses on the hawk's legs. The swivel prevents the jesses and leash becoming entangled when the bird moves off the perch. In the past, swivels were made of brass with a steel rivet. As a special corrosion-resistant steel was not used, in time the rivet would rust and it was possible for the bird to escape. In modern times, stronger and non-corrosive materials are used.

A device known as a 'lure' is offered in the field to tempt the hawk back to the ground after an unsuccessful flight, and then eventually onto the falconer's fist. Meat is usually used on the lure, which consists of a leather wad which is weighted and attached, via a swivel, to a strong linen cord about twelve feet long. The other end of the line is tied around a groove in the middle of a wooden grip for the falconer to hold. The line must be strong enough to resist the force of

A Hawking Party
(*A.F. De Prades*)

a hawk tugging at it without breaking.

The lure is swung through the air to simulate a wild quarry; in the past a dead bird was used. The trained hawk is attracted to the lure and settles on it on the ground. Often artificial feathered wings are attached to the lure but a shape resembling a pigeon's wings is not favoured by many falconers. This is because the hawks, when hunting, may be distracted by pigeons which are not only fairly numerous but also a very elusive quarry to catch. In the past, as was done similarly with their gloves, the Royals' lures were often highly decorated and finely embossed, despite the extreme harsh treatment they would have been subjected to if used in the field. They may therefore have been made purely for ornamental purposes and never used for practical falconry.

Hawks are not only trained differently from the long-winged falcons but are also handled differently in the field. In contrast to the falcon, the hawks are usually transported without a hood and the head is always kept uncovered when in the hunting field. However, hawks are more difficult to train and are more unpredictable than falcons. The buzzard is probably the easiest hawk to train and it is now one of the United Kingdom's most common large birds of prey. Despite its size, buzzards when flying are frequently mobbed by gulls or members of the crow family. Nowadays, many people start to learn falconry with a buzzard before progressing to a goshawk.

Patience is required in hawking, as often there is a delay in tempting the disappointed hawk, after missing its quarry, back to the lure. It often chooses to sit and perhaps sulk in a distant tree. It is essential always to retrieve the bird, as a trained hawk may not survive on its own in the wild. It has become tame and accustomed to man feeding it. The leather straps on the legs may also become entangled in a bush or tree and inhibit the hawk's chance of survival. Escaped tamed hawks do sometimes thrive and successfully breed but it is difficult to calculate the percentage. It is essential for the hawk to be well trained before it is released, so that the chance of it not returning to the lure is minimized. The lure has to be used frequently, as on average between fifty and sixty-five per cent of all flights result in the quarry not being killed and therefore it escapes unharmed. This means that the disappointed hawk has to be retrieved by the falconer.

Today, the Wildlife and Countryside Act of 1981 protects all wild hawks in the United Kingdom. Heavy penalties and fines await anyone found guilty of killing or taking them from the wild. The majority of falcons for sport are now therefore bred in captivity, although in certain cases the Secretary of State, through the Department of the Environment, can issue a special licence to allow a hawk to be taken from the wild, or imported from overseas for breeding purposes and for falconry. All captive hawks must be ringed and registered with the Department of the Environment, which has the power to inspect the premises of the hawk owner where the bird is housed.

Medieval kings, of course, took all their falcons from the wild, and from many different locations. They were so proud of their birds of prey that the falcons acompanied them on all their travels, and even to wars overseas. When Henry II was in Wales in 1171, planning to invade Ireland, one of his goshawks was killed by a wild peregrine falcon. He was greatly impressed by the feat and afterwards thought very highly of the ability of the peregrine. As a result, each year he sent an order for young peregrine falcons to be captured for him from the coastal cliffs of Pembrokeshire in Wales.

Henry II developed a liking for the falcons obtained from Norway and other areas of Scandinavia, which had gained a good reputation for the supply of birds of prey. He even established his falconer on his estates in Norfolk and Lincolnshire, so that he would be close to the trading which took place at St Botolph's Fair in Boston, Lincolnshire. This was the centre for the buying and selling of hawks from both Norway and the Mediterranean areas. The royal falconer also scrutinized the hawks entering the ports at Yarmouth and Lynn. Later, hawks were exchanged for East Anglian corn.

Hawks were often used during the twelfth and thirteenth centuries to settle outstanding debts, fines and other payments which were due to the king. Even as late as 1764, the system appeared to be still in favour, as the Dukes of Atholl discovered when they retained the tenancy of the Isle of Man. They had to pay their rent for the island to each succeeding monarch, when he came to the throne, in the form of two white gyrfalcons.

When John, the son of Henry II, became King in 1199, he often imported falcons from Ireland. In fact, falcons became so important to John that Nicholas the Dane later tried to bribe him with an offer of a regular supply of hawks, if he was allowed to trade other goods freely with England. Through the ensuing years, falconry received a boost from new birds which were brought back to England by the returning military expeditions from the various Eastern crusades. The sport still remains extremely popular in the East and the Saker falcon, sometimes known as the desert falcon, is now much favoured by Arab falconers.

Edward II preferred his hawks to be obtained from Norway and his son Edward III, in the fourteenth century, became a very keen falconer as well. He considered that the stealing of a hawk was such a serious offence that only the death penalty would suffice as a punishment. Edward III took about thirty falconers along with him when he invaded France, no doubt in order to pursue his passion for the sport between battles and to relax. During his reign, the clergy travelled with their hawks as a diversion from their pastoral duties. For instance, when the Bishop of Ely attended a service in the Great Abbey at Bermondsey, in Southwark, he left his hawk on a perch in the cloister. To his dismay, when he returned for it the bird had been stolen. The Bishop, without hesitation, solemnly excommunicated the thieves from the Church, although they were never caught to learn their fate. If they had been apprehended, they would have probably been put to death anyway for this act of felony.

Henry VII, when he was on the throne, initiated an early contribution to the concept of conservation by imprisoning anyone convicted of stealing or destroying falcons' eggs. This helped considerably in establishing a stable population of falcons in the wild, as previously the robbing of nests had caused their number to dwindle considerably. The royal patronage continued through the years and Henry VIII participated in both falconry and most forms of hunting with great zeal. The sport of falconry nearly cost Henry his life on one occasion, when he was hawking at Hitchin in Hertfordshire. He was following his bird and attempted to vault over a deep mud-filled ditch with a pole. The pole broke and the heavy king fell head-first into the thick, clinging quagmire. He might have smothered but for the quick action of one of his followers, who immediately dived into the ditch and managed to rescue him.

The height of popularity for the sport was probably reached in Elizabethan times. Mary Queen of Scots also relished hawking, especially with the merlin falcon, when on hunting expeditions in Scotland. Later, when she was imprisoned in England at Tutbury Castle, she still managed to ride with her falcons and she was even accompanied on occasions by the Royal Falconer of England. When Elizabeth I came to hear of these excursions she was most displeased and speedily halted them. James I, during his reign in the seventeenth century, wrote a treatise on the art of falconry and he favoured the falcons obtained from Denmark. Another favourite source for falcons was Valkenswaard, in Holland. It not only became a major trade centre for the birds but it also gained status as a good place to learn the art of falconry and to obtain the necessary equipment to pursue it.

After the execution of Charles I and during the Interregnum period, from 1649 to the Restoration of the Monarchy in 1660, the sport of falconry was seriously affected, although many people still used hawks to hunt for food. Many of the mews where the falcons were kept were closed down during the Civil War. The word 'mews' originally meant the cages or small buildings where falcons and hawks on the 'mew', or moult, were housed. Many of these mews were later converted, or rebuilt, as stables for horses. The word 'mews' then was used to denote horse stables around an open yard or along a path. Many of these stables have now been converted into garages or dwellings and are known as mews houses.

In London, on the site where the National Gallery now stands, on the north side of Charing Cross in Trafalgar Square, once stood the Royal Mews where the King's falcons were kept. It was utilized for two centuries for this purpose, dating from the fourteenth century when it was first established by Richard II. However, it was converted long before the Civil War into royal stables, to house the King's horses in the sixteenth century.

At the Restoration of the Monarchy, Charles II attempted to revive the sport of falconry and collected hawks for the purpose. James II tried to continue the process and made the succeeding Dukes of St Albans hereditary Grand Falconers from 1688. However, other indirect factors started to inhibit the growth of the sport during the following century and it suffered a serious decline by the end of the eighteenth century in England. The lack of royal support and the growing popularity of beagling and then fox-hunting were two reasons. Even more important was the development of the sporting gun for game shooting and the enclosure of land, both of which had severe adverse effects on falconry. The latter was a particular problem for the falconer, as the vast large open tracts of land were no longer available. The sport managed to survive in Scotland much longer than in England.

Despite the rapid decline of falconry in the eighteenth century, George II still kept hawks and his son Frederick, Prince of Wales, often flew his birds on Epsom Downs. In an attempt to keep the sport strong, various Falconers' Clubs were formed. One of the first was the Falconers' Society of England, founded around 1770. It claimed between fifty and sixty members by 1781 and the club organized an annual event at a selected venue in East Anglia. Alconbury Hill in Huntingdonshire became an established favourite meeting place. In 1792 a small group formed the High Ash Club in Norfolk, and its first president was Lord Orford. The club employed professional falconers who came from Denmark, and it prospered until the 1830s. The members chiefly used peregrine falcons to hunt herons. The club was disbanded after its president Lord Berners died. The number of herons had been declining, and it also became more difficult to ride with falcons, because of changes in the agricultural management of land and larger areas under the plough.

The keen falconers from England and especially the aristocratic ones journeyed to Holland to hunt herons. They joined forces with the Dutch and formed the Loo Hawking Club in 1839. This Anglo-Dutch Society was honoured with the royal patronage of King William II of the Netherlands and it prospered for many years. However, the

membership declined, along with the royal support, and the club was eventually disbanded in 1853. Many enthusiastic amateurs tried to revive the sport in England immediately afterwards and they were assisted by a few professional falconers. In 1864, the Old Hawking Club of England was founded by them. This continued until 1926 and the club had its own headquarters, professional falconers and their own hawks. Most members of the club were more interested in the art of falconry than in the hunting of game birds. They were quite content to hunt rooks on the downs of Wiltshire.

After the Old Hawking Club disbanded in 1926, some keen members formed The British Falconers' Club in the following year (1927). No professional falconers were employed and the club was kept strictly amateur. Members trained and flew their own birds, which were goshawks. Most could not afford the time to give the large amount of exercise needed to keep peregrine falcons fit. After the

A Hawking Party with Hawk Carrier (*James Ross*)

Second World War, the club was reduced to just a few members. The decline was due to several factors but the chief one was the grave shortage of hawks. The British Falconers' Club continued to function but many of the members did not practise hunting. In the 1950s and 1960s, the club had a membership of about two hundred and fifty, but the number who flew hawks was only around twelve per cent. The club still exists.

One reason for the shortage of hawks and falcons, amongst many others, was The Destruction of Peregrine Falcons Order 1940, initiated by the Secretary of State for Air under Regulation 9 of the Defence (General) Regulations 1939. This order was made to exterminate peregrine falcons in certain localities, where they might have killed carrier-pigeons used by the military to fly with urgent wartime messages.

Another indirect cause was myxomatosis which spread throughout the United Kingdom in 1954 and almost wiped out the rabbit population of over 60 million. The disease gravely reduced the potential food supply for predators such as hawks, and many birds died. In addition, many goshawks had already been exterminated in England by a long history of persecution by gamekeepers, due to the hawks' attacks on game-birds. Despite this, a few goshawks continued to breed naturally in Sussex until 1951 but eventually they succumbed to the gamekeepers' guns or were driven off their nesting sites. The felling of forests and the destruction of hedgerows also led to a further decline, due to the loss of habitat for hawks and their prey.

The goshawk is one of the world's largest true hawks with a wingspan of up to four feet. These birds stand up to two feet high and the larger female weighs up to 4 lb. In the wild, goshawks are determined hunters and attack their prey with speed, agility, power and surprise, using their great talons. From an agricultural point of view, they play a beneficial role in controlling the numbers of magpies, woodpigeons, rabbits and vermin. Unfortunately, they also kill a large number of game- and song-birds. However, the large conifer forests planted in recent years in the United Kingdom have allowed goshawks to start breeding again. They were re-introduced from northern Europe and Scandinavia. There are now thought to be around two hundred and fifty pairs of goshawks. Sadly, attempts have been made to steal the eggs, so the nests have to be guarded or their location kept secret.

With regard to the peregrine falcon, a fairly strong population had been re-established in the United Kingdom by the middle of the 1950s, after their earlier decline due to the gamekeepers' guns. However, their numbers had rapidly deteriorated again by 1962, when some estimated that there were as few as about seventy pairs of peregrines left in the whole of the United Kingdom. Other more optimistic estimates suggested a higher figure of about three hundred and fifty pairs. This decline was due to the indirect poisoning of the birds by the agricultural pesticide, dieldrin, which got into the food chain. The same chemical was also responsible for the deaths of large numbers of goshawks, sparrowhawks and buzzards.

Dieldrin is an organic chlorine compound, used as a pesticidal coating on seeds which were often eaten by woodpigeons, the prey of the falcon and other hawks. Each time a peregrine falcon ate a woodpigeon, a small amount of dieldrin entered its body and was stored in the fat tissue. With the passage of time, the chemical reached a critical accumulated dose in the peregrine's body and this often proved fatal. Sometimes the poison just made the bird infertile, or the eggs it laid possessed very thin shells. This last problem presented a big hazard to the chicks' chances of survival. Fortunately, the use of dieldrin as an agricultural chemical was controlled in 1964 and this assisted in the slow re-establishment of both falcon and hawk populations. The existing groups of peregrine falcons are now chiefly confined to the extreme northern and western coasts of the United Kingdom, although they are occasionally found in other areas. It is thought that the total number of peregrine falcons has probably increased since the 1960s to about a thousand pairs by the 1990s.

Despite the decline in the number of wild birds of prey, the establishment of the Falconry Centre at Newent, Gloucestershire has played a major role in the conservation of the sport of falconry in England. The Centre not only breeds birds in captivity but also teaches the art of falconry. Exhibitions and falconry courses are now available in many other areas of England. Also, the existing British Falconers' Club has issued a code of conduct for practising hawkers, now reduced to a small band of enthusiasts. The few of these who indulge in game-hawking find it extremely expensive owing to the high costs of sporting rights. In addition, the falconers can only pursue their quarry during the permitted season for game-birds. Under the Wildlife and Countryside Act many wild species are now protected, although hares, rabbits and classified vermin, such as rats and grey squirrels, may be taken at any time without restriction. However, in all cases permission is required from the owner, or his representative, to fly a hawk over his land. Without permission, hawking becomes a poaching offence.

In the vast majority of flights today, the falconer uses only a single hawk, whilst in the past it was quite common to fly a 'cast' or a pair at the same time. The falconer may fly his hawk either from the ground, or occasionally when mounted on horseback. In the latter case, the lengthy period required to train the hawk and build up trust is further extended as hawk, horse and man all have to work together as a team.

Although peregrine falcons can be flown at an enormous variety of game-birds, they do require very open territory to be effective. Nowadays, the grouse moors provide the best locations. The long-winged falcon is particularly suited to hunting the higher and faster-flying game-birds, such as the grouse and partridge. In these cases, the falcon is assisted by a hawking dog, such as a setter or pointer. The dog searches the moor until it scents a covey. It then stands still and 'points' the hidden bird to the falconer, who releases the falcon. The bird immediately climbs up in a spiral flight-path until it reaches its 'pitch' several hundred feet up, where it waits overhead of the indicated covey.

The dog then flushes the grouse into the air, when the falconer signals, and the falcon flies two or three small circles before it commences its high-speed stoop or dive at its flying quarry. The speed of the peregrine dive may reach up to ninety miles per hour. The prey may turn to avoid the stoop, if it senses the attack, but if it is unsuccessful the falcon strikes the flying bird with its talons with such tremendous force that the quarry is usually dead before it hits the ground. The falcon then settles on the dead bird and the falconer approaches quietly. He places both the falcon and its dead prey on his gloved fist and allows the falcon to eat a tiny piece of its victim, as a reward for its successful flight. He then takes the prey away.

Instead of hunting for game-birds, sometimes the falcon may be flown at smaller prey such as crows, rooks, gulls and other less prestigious quarry. In this case, the falcon is often flown direct by removing the hood whilst on the fist, so that it immediately sees the quarry. The falcon climbs above it and circles a few times, using any available wind to increase speed, before descending with its fast final attack on its selected victim. Again, the falcon will hit its quarry when it is in the air.

In contrast to the long-winged peregrine, the short-winged hawks such as the goshawk, buzzard or sparrowhawk have the advantage of being able to hunt in more wooded and enclosed territory. In this case, the falconer walks with his hawk on the fist and is accompanied by a dog such as a spaniel, which searches the undergrowth and hedgerows. When a rabbit, for example, bolts from its cover the hawk immediately leaves the fist and flies swiftly at it by the shortest possible route. The prey is seized by the very strong talons of the hawk and is quickly killed. If the hawk fails in its attack, it will settle on the branch of a nearby tree or a fence post and wait. Sometimes, instead of flying the hawk from the fist, it is allowed to follow the falconer and his spaniel by hopping from tree to tree until a potential quarry is found and flushed out by the dog for the hawk. The quarry may not always be a rabbit, as occasionally pheasants, hares and other small animals may be caught. Most modern falconry now takes place over typical farmland rather than on the more exclusive grouse moors. The average number of kills made by a hawk in a season normally ranges between fifty and a hundred.

Despite the vastly changed nature of the countryside from that in medieval times, the basics of falconry have stayed almost as they were five hundred years ago. The birds are the same, although the goshawk is now more frequently trained than the peregrine falcon. The falconer spends far less time in the company of his bird than his medieval predecessors. Most of the equipment has suffered little change, although obviously modern technology has allowed improvements to be made and better materials to be used in manufacture.

4 Stag and Deer Hunting

In medieval times, deer were extensively hunted for food but only by the favoured few. Even before William I (the Conqueror) reigned, vast areas of land had already been reserved for the exclusive hunting by King Canute in the early eleventh century. Large tracts of land at Epping, Windsor and Huntingdon were classified as Royal Forests under protection of the law. Those who infringed the royal rights of the hunt were severely punished.

The Normans vastly extended the forest areas and by the end of the thirteenth century, forests covered more than a third of the total area of England. Expanses of heath and moorland formed parts of the forest tracts. The Normans created over eighty Royal Forests and they included not only Epping, Windsor and Huntingdon but many others such as Sherwood, the Forest of Dean, Exmoor and perhaps the most famous of all, the New Forest. Originally the New Forest was called the Nova Foresta; it was decreed a Royal Forest by William I in 1079 and later an additional sixty-nine acres were added. William I initiated Forest Laws to ensure that the King's right to hunt took precedence over all other matters. Anyone illegally hunting deer risked having their arms and feet cut off or their eyes plucked out.

The Normans reserved not only the deer and other beasts of the chase for the court and nobility but the timber also became royal property, although commoners were granted permission to graze their livestock and gather mainly dead vegetation such as small branches, reeds, brushwood, bracken and hay. Many of these old commoners' rights still exist in the New Forest, as evidenced by their grazing rights for cattle and ponies, together with the Court of Verderers who adjudicate over them.

In the establishment of the Royal Forests, a few villagers were forcibly expelled, their churches closed and the villages abandoned. However, the majority of the settlements remained in the forest. Norman kings spent a considerable time hunting, so it was convenient to build many of their castles with their estates and manors adjacent to or within the forests. Examples are Windsor,

A Stag Hunt of Former
Times (*F. Desportes*)

Nottingham, Northampton and Marlborough. In addition, many
hunting lodges were established in the forests. However, with the
passage of time and the signing of the Magna Carta, the vast
stretches of Royal Forest were gradually reduced in size but it was
not until the Restoration period that the harsh Forest Laws were
finally abolished.

The male red deer, the stag, was the prime quarry hunted by the
Royals but the hind (the female red deer), the buck (the male roe
deer) and the wild boar were pursued as well. The forests also

harboured wolves which were hunted, and these survived in England until about 1500. They survived much longer in Scotland, until about 1740, and in Ireland to about 1770. With the extinction of the wolf, the only natural predator of the deer was removed; the lynx, its only other natural predator, probably became extinct during the early post-glacial period. A male red deer was classified as a stag when it reached the age of five but in Norman times it was not usually hunted until it was deemed to be six. It was then called a hart and was the aristocrat of the chase. When the King hunted a particular hart, it became known as a 'hart royal'. If the hart royal escaped out of the Royal Forest and wandered further afield, a protection order or proclamation was placed on it by the King which forbade anyone killing or harming the animal. The escaped hart royal was then called a 'hart royal proclaimed'. The protection was granted in case the deer one day returned to the Royal Forest.

Although the chase was conducted at a slow pace, there were many hunting accidents. William the Conqueror lost three of his descendants at different times while they were out hunting in the New Forest. A stag gored to death his eldest son Richard, and a nephew of one of his other sons, Rufus, was crushed against a tree by a horse which panicked. The third and the most well-known hunting accident was that of Rufus himself (so-called because of his flame-coloured hair), after he became William II.

The story of his death remains shrouded in mystery. One suggestion is that it may have been deliberately arranged by his younger brother, who succeeded him as Henry I. It is undisputed that he was killed by a hunting arrow in August 1100, near to the turnpike road which linked Lymington to Salisbury. At the time he was sheltering in a covert in a dell, awaiting the appearance of a stag, and he was alone with a French knight, Sir William Tyrrel. The remainder of the hunting party were much further away in the forest, so there were no eye-witnesses to the exact event which was to unfold. It was assumed that the French knight fired his crossbow at a stag which suddenly emerged from cover and the arrow ricocheted off a tree and struck Rufus.

Apparently, the French knight hastily departed from the scene and galloped away to the nearest port to return to France. He immediately joined a Crusade which was departing to the East. It was suggested the death may have been a conspiracy rather than an accident. However, the knight would have been terrified of retribution even if he was innocent, and this may have been the reason for his desertion. The body of Rufus was later found by a forester, called Purkiss, who worked as a charcoal burner. He was travelling through the forest when he stumbled upon the body of Rufus and he carried him back on his cart to Winchester Palace. The tomb of William Rufus can still be seen in Winchester Cathedral.

The charcoal burner later received two acres of land as a reward for his service; the descendants of Purkiss inherited the land and continued the trade of charcoal burning in the New Forest for many generations. The oak tree where the accident occurred was later named the Rufus Oak but unfortunately it died prematurely due to the keenness of souvenir hunters cutting pieces from it. A fragment of the root of the oak was preserved and the site in the New Forest where he died is now marked with the 'Rufus Stone'.

The Normans when they arrived in England introduced a style of hunting which became known as 'par force' or 'hunting by force'. It used horsemen and hounds in relays and the quarry was unhampered in the direction of its flight, or the distance it covered. This type of hunting was initially the reserve of royalty but later members of the Church were allowed to participate. Eventually, the clergy were prohibited from owning hounds under threat of imprisonment. This was reputedly due to the influence of moralists but probably more so to the number of the King's deer they were taking. Henry II admonished them for wasting their time in the forest, although he himself spent most of his own time in the hunting field. Despite the ban, many of the clergy were not above a little poaching; for example, the local abbot was convicted of trespassing and poaching in the Forest of Peterborough. Henry III, when he came to the throne in the thirteenth century, was a keen huntsman like his predecessors and he issued orders to the sheriffs that they should keep all the bridges in their shires in good repair, to assist his hunting expeditions.

One story relates that whilst hunting in Dorset, Henry III's party pursued a white hart all day through the Forest of Blackmore without success. The King admired the beast so much that he decreed it must never he hunted again. Later, a band of huntsmen disobeyed the order and the white stag was killed. King Henry was so incensed that he fined and heavily taxed the Blackmore Estates from which the offending huntsmen came. This tax was claimed annually until the seventeenth century, and the money became known as 'White Hart Silver'. The symbol of the White Hart was incorporated into several coats-of-arms and the name became a popular one for many taverns with hunting connections.

The hounds used in Norman times were not precise breeds but were broader types comprising various sizes for different functions in the hunting field. Later, the original French breeds were crossed with native hounds. The lymers, as they were known, had excellent scenting ability and were used to track the stag. They were held on a nine-foot-long, highly decorated leash, made of horse hide, which was called a 'liam'. When they had successfully found a stag, the lymers

Hound Coursing a
Buck

were led away and the so-called running hounds brought forward and
released for the actual chase, or *la chasse* as it was termed by the
French.

The running hounds, or 'raches', such as Talbots and Gascons,
were heavy and powerfully built and therefore relatively slow in the
chase. Each was large enough to pull down a deer. Legend claims
that they were descended from the original hounds bred by St
Hubert. In the sixth century St Hubert was the patron saint of
hunting. The Normans also used greyhounds which were variable in
size and type of coat. They were fast and hunted by sight. The 'alaunt'
or mastiff was used to pursue wolves, as well as deer and boar,
because of the dog's size and great power.

The running hounds hunted the stag until it was brought down or
more usually held at bay. The reason that a stag stood at bay with the
hounds around was a defensive mechanism developed in its
evolutionary days, to counter its natural predator, the wolf. The stag
normally elected to stand on a spot on a steep slope or in water, so
that it could effectively use its antlers to ward off its attackers. In
Norman times, the stag at bay was usually killed by an arrow and the

task completed with a sword or knife. The ritual developed that the most important person present was given the honour of using the blade. This was normally the King and this practice continued through the following centuries. For example, James I in the seventeenth century not only cut the throat of the stag but started the fashion of daubing the faces of courtiers with the blood, which they were not allowed to wash off.

The actual hunt procedure, known as the art of venery or the science of hunting, was a slow chase based on French etiquette, and the language of the chase was initially always Norman French. The chase only became faster when the fox was hunted in the eighteenth century. William Twici wrote an early treatise entitled *Le Art de Venerie* in about 1328, which was later translated into English. Other works on the art of venery followed but perhaps the most famous was the *Boke of St Albans*, reputedly written by Dame Juliana Berners in 1486. The five 'wild beasts of venery' were the hart, the hind, the hare, the boar and the wolf. It became essential to be always correct in the hunting field and all the published works were studied and followed by the rich in order not to damage their social position.

The royal beasts of the chase were mainly the red and the roe deer, which were native to Britain. Both were woodland creatures but later had to adapt to more open areas when large tracts of forest were felled. When living in the forest, the deer caused damage by eating herbs and the foliage of the broadleaf trees. This is perhaps why the Normans prevented the commoners from felling or taking branches away, as this amounted to removing potential food from the mouths of the deer. The Normans were responsible for the re-introduction of the fallow deer into England during the eleventh century and later into Ireland in 1244. They released them into the forests to join the native red and roe deer and to become eventually themselves highly prized quarries to hunt during the following centuries. The original herds of fallow deer in the British Isles died out during the Ice Age, although a few may have been brought back to England by the Romans.

The Normans developed the concept of the medieval deer parks which were enclosed by a stout deer fence or a high earth bank. The fence was constructed of long vertical oak stakes, driven close together into the ground and nailed to a horizontal joining rail. The parks were substantial, covering vast tracts of land, and most were therefore large enough to allow hunting within the surrounding ring-fence. On occasions, the Normans would allow deer to escape from the park so that they could be hunted 'at force' in the traditional way. These releases into the countryside must have been inconvenient to the ordinary poor people who lived in the surrounding area of the deer park. No doubt, in return they must have been very tempted to indulge in a little poaching, with such a concentration of deer in the nearby enclosure.

Most deer parks in the thirteenth century were owned by rich upper-class members of society and their status was much enhanced if they managed to obtain a royal licence from the King to construct a deer-leap on the perimeter of their park. All wild deer belonged to the King but if you were favoured by him, and for the payment of a substantial licence fee, permission for the construction of a deer-leap was sometimes granted. This was a complicated arrangement of banks and ditches which allowed a wild deer to pass into a deer park but not out again. It was a one-way system. The outbreak of plague which later hit England during the fourteenth century killed so many men that most of the fences around the deer parks were no longer maintained and many deer escaped.

During the sixteenth century, much improved versions of the early Norman deer parks evolved. These were landscaped parks achieved by the carefully designed enclosure of land by the richer squirearchy of English society. They were situated by their manor houses and the parks were used exclusively for hunting with a pack of hounds. Both the ladies and the gentlemen of the household followed the hounds. Many of the more wealthy families owned two deer parks, one for red deer and the other for fallow deer. The Civil War which broke out in the following century caused many of these parks to fall into disuse and again many deer escaped, as the fences were broken down.

In the eighteenth century, deer parks were in fashion again and they became an essential part of a stately home. They typified the English gentility and several were later further improved by Capability Brown, the celebrated English landscape gardener. He acquired his nickname by frequently telling his clients that their grounds had 'capabilities for landscape development'. Many of these deer parks are still in existence today, despite the frequent escapes of deer during the two World Wars of the twentieth century. The majority of the wild fallow deer at large in England today are direct descendants of the escapees from deer parks during the past centuries. For example, the few remaining fallow deer on Exmoor are descendants of escapees from the former deer parks at Dunster Castle and Nettlecombe Court. During the nineteenth century, sika, muntjak and Chinese water deer were additionally introduced into the deer parks but many of these also have since escaped to join the fallow deer in the wild.

As well as hunting a single deer 'at force', it was also popular with the monarchs to hunt deer by coursing. In this sport, a number of deer would be coursed or driven by hounds, accompanied usually by three mounted men, to pass by a pre-arranged spot in a covert, where stands had been erected for the King and Queen together with invited nobility. Sometimes carriages were drawn up alongside for

Stag Hunting (*James Ross*)

the ladies. The archers shot with their crossbows at the relatively easy targets when they ran into the ambush and any deer which escaped the hail of arrows were frequently pursued with greyhounds. Unlike hunting 'at force', coursing of deer resulted in the death of many deer at the same time. It was a barbarous activity and there was little chance for the quarry to escape.

An example of such a deer shooting stand still survives at Chingford, in Ranger's Road, on the edge of Epping Forest. It dates from the sixteenth century and was used as a hunting lodge by Queen Elizabeth I. It has two storeys but the top one remains open to the sky and it was from here the archers shot the deer. Earlier, Henry VIII used Richmond Park in Surrey for similar activities and he stood on a mound at the highest point to acquire a good vantage point during the deer-hunting drives. He also used the Epping Forest lodge.

In the reign of Elizabeth I, a new type of deer coursing was introduced, known as 'paddock coursing'. This involved the construction of a course about a mile long with high rails along each side to contain the deer on the chosen track. The rails were placed so that the course gradually widened from start to finish, in order that the spectators could have a better view at the finish, where the stands were erected. Again the deer were driven up the course and shot with crossbows.

Later, paddock coursing developed into a somewhat more humane sport, using greyhounds to pursue the deer but without the archers lying in wait. In this type, four posts were positioned along the course

Stag at Bay

at distances of 160 yards, 440 yards, 880 yards and about one mile. The first post was called the 'law post' and the final post the 'pinching post'. A deer was driven up to the start of the course and one greyhound was released to entice it to run faster. When the speeding deer reached the first post, a couple of greyhounds were 'slipped' to chase after it. There were detailed rules but in essence the dog closest to the deer at the finishing post was the winner. It later became usual to construct a ditch at the end of the course, so that the deer could be trapped and the dogs prevented from reaching it. The spectators gained extra excitement from coursing by wagering on the result.

Queen Elizabeth I much preferred to hunt the deer on horseback, rather than in static paddock coursing. As well as the Royal Forests, she hunted in St James's Park, Hyde Park and Regent's Park which were then hunting grounds. In the course of her expeditions her party would stop for lavish picnics when resting during the hunt. She used to fire with a heavy crossbow and rode to hounds when over seventy years of age. A later lady huntress, Queen Anne, was an equally keen horsewoman. When in the early eighteenth century she became older and somewhat more plump, she insisted on following the hounds but in a special single-seated horse-drawn carriage. This resembled a narrow chariot with high wheels and she drove it furiously in Windsor Forest over the roughest terrain during the deer hunt.

The crossbow was used more for hunting than the longbow, especially by the ladies; although the longbow could be shot at a faster rate than the crossbow it required more strength to draw. The longbow had been developed in the thirteenth century by the Welsh tribes to antagonise Edward I's military forces. Later it was exploited by the English for warfare, as exemplified by the archers at Crécy and Agincourt. Initially longbows were made of elm but yew was substituted because of its better external rigidity and internal suppleness.

The Elizabethan reign saw the beginnings of the modern method of carefully selecting a particular stag to chase, rather than finding one more randomly to hunt in relays. The technique of hunting hind and buck was also established. The Earl of Leicester kept the Queen's buckhounds at Kenilworth, whilst her staghounds were kennelled at Simonsbath on Exmoor to hunt the red deer. Hugh Pollard was believed to be the keeper of the staghounds in 1598. The royal staghounds hunted on Exmoor for over two centuries but were later reformed as the Devon and Somerset Staghounds. The Stuart monarchs not only kept established packs of royal hounds but were keen to increase the number of deer to hunt. For this purpose, William III imported over a hundred red deer from Germany for release into Windsor Forest in the seventeenth century.

The royal packs of hounds were finally disbanded by Edward VII at the beginning of this century. This was not because of his lack of enthusiasm for sport but because he preferred other types. In fact, his sporting interests increased his popularity with his subjects. His racing yacht *Britannia* brought great prestige and he was the first reigning monarch to be successful in the English Derby, when his racehorse Minoru won in 1909.

It was the eighteenth century that brought adverse changes for the hunting of deer. Forest clearance to increase pastureland had reduced the number of wild deer. Large tracts of oak forest had already been felled to provide timber for the shipbuilding industry. This had started in the seventeenth century. The demand was vast; for example, the construction of a single 'man o' war' devoured about three thousand large oak trees. There was no systematic forestry replacement programme in the seventeenth century and much of the deer's natural habitat was destroyed.

This led to the near extinction of the native deer in England by the beginning of the eighteenth century, as they were almost entirely woodland animals. Fortunately an increase in woodland planting helped their numbers to expand slightly by the end of the century. This applied especially to Scotland and northern England. In the south, an improvement was achieved by the re-introduction of the roe deer to the region. For instance, a complete herd was transferred to Milton Abbas, in Dorset, around 1800. In the 1920s, the development of new forestry plantations further assisted the growth of the roe deer population in southern England. Although previously hunted, the roe deer escaped further pursuit and there has been no large-scale hunting of roe deer with hounds in England since the beginning of the nineteenth century.

The general scarcity of wild deer helped hare and fox-hunting to become more popular in the eighteenth century. These were done either on foot with hounds or on horse with hounds. Fox-hunting demanded a smaller, faster hound to complement the more active and faster nature of the sport. The large English staghound of the Gascon breed was allowed to die out gradually and the last true pack was exported at the beginning of the nineteenth century. It was purchased by a German baron. All hounds hunting deer this century now derive from foxhound origins.

At the beginning of the eighteenth century, London was still quite rural and in one incident a stag was even bayed by hounds in Bloomsbury, by the site of the present British Museum. This occurred outside Number 1 Montague Street, which adjoins the museum. Staghounds hunted around the Twickenham, Richmond and Hounslow districts well into the nineteenth century.

Another feature of the early eighteenth century was the start of the

Sportsman Stalking
Two Deer (*Ridinger*)

hunting of carted deer; that is, deer transported in a cart to wooded countryside to be hunted. It is thought that the sport commenced around 1725, when carted elk were pursued in Windsor Park. Later, George III enjoyed the sport and kept five deer paddocks at Swinley. Both stags and hinds were transported from the paddock to the meeting to be chased by him and his guests but it was done purely for entertainment; the deer were never killed.

The carted deer eventually became very tame and sometimes they even travelled in the same conveyance as the hounds. When a deer was turned loose, it would sometimes refuse to run and would just graze or even get back into the vehicle again to be taken home. This obviously ruined the hunt unless another deer was taken as a reserve. If it ran the deer was given a fair start before the hounds were released and the hunt commenced. The chase was usually run at a good pace and in time the stag would stop and stand its ground at bay with the hounds. It was then lassoed, or if really tame a halter was placed on its head to lead it back to the conveyance for the journey home.

Carted deer hunting no longer takes place in England. In the past it was always most popular in regions near to cities or towns. The fringe of London, such as the Vale of Putney, was the territory of the Surrey Staghounds. The Norwich staghound pack was one of the very last to operate, up to the end of the 1960s. One advantage of the hunting of carted deer was that the chase was normally fast and therefore over in a relatively short time. It did not entail the pursuit of the quarry over many miles of wild country and for many hours.

Although carted deer hunting is a thing of the past, four separate packs of hounds survive into the 1990s to hunt wild deer. Three of these operate on Exmoor and the neighbouring Quantocks to hunt the red deer. The oldest, the Devon and Somerset Staghounds (founded in 1853) have their hunt stables and kennels at Exford in the centre of Exmoor. These were built in 1875 at the instigation of the long-serving Master, Fenwick Bisset. At the present time, the hunt still thrives and owns about thirty horses and sixty-five couples of hounds. The Quantock Staghounds (founded in 1920) also operate in the region and the Tiverton Staghounds (founded in 1896) hunt the red deer in both North Devon and West Somerset.

The fourth pack, The New Forest Buckhounds (founded in 1854), hunt the fallow deer of the New Forest, under licence from the deputy surveyor, appointed by the Forestry Commission. The Commission administers the Forest as agent of the Crown. The fallow deer are now the most widespread species of deer in the British Isles but it is only the male of the species, the buck, which is hunted with hounds in the New Forest. However, the hunt kills relatively few deer, the population being chiefly culled by stalking and shooting.

The red deer is the largest of Britain's mammals and a mature stag stands around four feet at the shoulder and weighs about 300 lb. The hind is smaller and stands three feet and normally weighs less than 200 lb. As mentioned earlier, although originally a woodland animal, the loss of forest habitat forced it to adapt to living in more open territory. It now survives not only on Exmoor and in the south west of

Sir Walter Scott Deer Stalking (*Sir Edwin Landseer*)

England but also in parts of northern Cumbria and Norfolk. The open moorland of the Scottish Highlands also carries large numbers.

The red deer living on Exmoor are the descendants of those that originally inhabited the moor when it was a Royal Forest. It is believed there are around fifteen hundred to two thousand adult deer remaining in the West Country. There is also a deer sanctuary on Exmoor owned by The League Against Cruel Sports. Deer cause considerable damage to crops on Exmoor by laying-up in cornfields and eating produce, especially when the winter is harsh. Some farmers grow a little extra to compensate for the loss. The deer also make considerable inroads into the supply of early spring grass destined for farm stock and silage. Most farmers tolerate the damage and support stag hunting by personally taking an active part. A culling of the numbers to eliminate the weak, the old and the sick is considered by most naturalists to be essential for the maintenance of the overall health of the herd in the long term. If the population grew too large, starvation and disease would result. The Red Deer Commission recommends a cull rate of one in six to stabilize the population.

A small cull is additionally done by shooting with a rifle but the nearness of unfenced woodland on Exmoor makes it more difficult to ensure that an animal does not escape wounded and therefore allowed to suffer. If it escapes injured onto someone else's land then it cannot be followed legally because of the risk of armed trespass. Exmoor attracts many visitors to its open expanses and any shooting, even using a rifle with telescopic sights, would have to be undertaken with caution. The cost of erecting deer fencing at least six feet high on Exmoor would not only be financially untenable to the many smallholders but would be visually detrimental on environmental grounds to the great beauty of Exmoor. However, a very small number of deer fences do exist and the first one ever erected was in 1898 by the Earl of Lovelace. The dilemma therefore presents itself of how best to control the red deer population. The farmers generally prefer the hunt, as this tends to break up large herds into smaller groups. The latter are more manageable if they get into a farmer's field. The farmers call on the hunt to despatch any injured or sick deer they may find on their land.

The National Trust in 1993 rejected a call for a ban on deer hunting on their property. They endorsed a two-year inquiry which concluded that hunting on Exmoor and the Quantock Hills in Somerset was of 'critical importance' to the welfare of red deer and the preservation of their habitat. They did not consider the ethical question of hunting owing to the conviction that this could only properly be solved in Parliament. The National Trust is the largest single landowner on Exmoor and controls around twenty thousand acres, including the wooded areas at Dunkery and Horner Wood, where most of the red deer are to be found.

There are no deer on neighbouring Dartmoor owing to the earlier slaughter carried out by farmers and poachers. In 1818, the Royal Forest of Exmoor was sold by the Crown and farming increased with the introduction of some enclosures. As a consequence, hunting with staghounds was discontinued on Exmoor from around 1825 to 1855. This nearly led to a similar situation as that on Dartmoor and the red deer population on Exmoor fell to below fifty, again owing to excessive poaching and shooting. It slowly increased again in the years after 1855, when hunting was revived and the many poachers for venison were frightened away. The farmers also curtailed their shooting and tolerated damage to their crops as the price for being able to hunt again. It may seem strange but the fact remains that the hunting of the red deer has played a powerful role in its conservation on Exmoor.

The seasons allowed for deer hunting are strictly controlled and are set by statutes laid down by Acts of Parliament. The season for hinds is from 1st November to the end of February. This is to ensure the hinds are not culled when they have dependent calves to feed at foot. The spring young stag hunting season starts in the middle of March and continues until the end of April. The spring hunt is confined to young stags of poor quality from three to five years old. The autumn mature stag hunt commences on 10th August and continues until 10th October, at which time the rut (the mating season) is due to begin. During the permitted seasons, it is illegal to kill or take any deer from one hour after sunset to one hour before sunrise on any day. Every effort is made to cull only the weakest and poorest animals, during the hind and young stag hunt seasons. This is what nature intended the wolf to do in earlier times. This ensured that only the healthiest males and females continued to breed, which increased the overall quality of the herd. In the case of hinds it is not necessary to select a particular animal, as the hounds normally achieve this task. The herd is chased and usually the adult hind in poorest condition breaks away from the herd as it cannot maintain the pace. When the deer eventually comes to a halt it stands at bay with the hounds. Unlike fox and hare hunting where the hounds make the kill, all deer are always shot at point-blank range by the huntsman, in the head or neck with an approved weapon (humane killer). The deer dies instantaneously and never escapes wounded as it may occasionally do if shot at long range with a rifle.

A different technique is used in the hunting of mature stags, as a particular beast is always selected and pursued. A day, or several hours, before a hunt commences, the harbourer, a hunt servant, carefully selects the stag which he considers to be one of the oldest or

Pony with a Dead Stag
(*J.F. Herring, Sen.*)

weakest. He bases his choice on a combination of experience, local knowledge or advice of farmers (he may be a farmer himself), the antler size of the stag and especially its physical condition. The footprint or slot of the animal gives the harbourer a clue as to its age and condition. The antlers also help to reveal the age. This is important as only warrantable stags at least five years old are considered to be a fair quarry. The harbourer, when assessing the stag after tracking it to its covert, must not allow it to sense his presence or it will move position before the hunt commences. When the hunt gets under way, only the selected 'harboured stag' is followed and all the others are disregarded by the huntsman.

At the start, the huntsman separates the harboured stag from any others by using just a few hounds, usually three or four couples. These older, experienced hounds have excellent scenting powers and are known as tufters. They carry out a similar function to their earlier forebears, the lymers of Norman times. Once the tufters achieve the task of getting the stag into the open, they are withdrawn and the rest of the pack, which were kept away, are 'laid on' for the chase.

The length of the hunt depends on many factors, such as the weather conditions and the scent. The deer will normally get well ahead of the hounds, as flight is the first instinct of defence. It will then slow down a little and the hounds follow the scent. Later it may stand its ground when it becomes tired, and adopt its second line of defence by instinctively standing at bay with the hounds around. The hounds respect the antlers and keep their distance. The stag is then despatched by the huntsman when he arrives on the scene. The huntsman during the hunt is assisted by the whippers-in to keep the hounds together. The rest of the field are all followers of the hunt. They enjoy the exercise, the fresh air and watching the hounds work. The huntsman carries the hunting horn to control the hounds; this is much more compact than the larger variety used by stag hunters in France. The French hunting horns were even larger in the eighteenth century.

In order to preserve the meat, the dead animal's throat must be cut to allow the blood to drain away. In Scotland, the term 'gralloch' describes the act of removing the internal organs from the carcass to prevent spoiling the edible flesh. The procedures follow similar lines to those used in a slaughterhouse, after any animal has been killed. Traditionally, in stag hunting the offal is given to the hounds as their prize. The trophy of the head of the stag goes to the farmer or landowner who has most strongly supported the day's hunt. The Master presents the venison, with his compliments, to the local farmers who have participated or over whose land the deer was hunted. Non-hunting farmers receive venison as well, if damage has accidentally occurred to their property. They also receive other forms of compensation.

The alternative method of stag hunting, known as deer stalking, is more suitable where the countryside is open and any nearby wooded areas are enclosed by fences. Again, the deer is shot but with a rifle, usually fitted with a telescopic sight to improve accuracy. The shooting takes place at a relatively long range compared with the short-range method of the humane killer employed in stag hunting with hounds. In deer stalking, rifles of over 0.24 inches calibre are used, and shotguns are never employed.

In England, unlike Scotland, stalking takes place over more wooded terrain. It therefore demands a different technique and involves much less climbing than in the Highlands. The hunting in England revolves mainly around the forest-dwelling deer, the fallow and to a more limited extent the roe. Woodland stalking became popular in England especially after the Second World War and the actual stalk with the rifle takes a much shorter time than the equivalent sport in Scotland. The possibility of losing a wounded deer arises but the risk is reduced as the animal can usually be followed. This is because the hunting terrain is not over a patchwork of smallholdings as is the case in Exmoor. The stalk normally takes place on a large estate under single ownership or management.

In earlier times in Scotland and to a more limited extent in England, the deerhounds were used to stalk deer and course them in open country. They could hold the deer at bay or even bring a stag down to the ground, by seizing the foreleg when running alongside. They could also kill quickly by biting the throat of the quarry when it rolled over. Deerhounds resembled greyhounds in appearance but had harsher and more wiry coats. They were very fast in pursuit and their keen sense of smell gave them excellent tracking abilities. The origin of deerhounds can be traced back to the early sixteenth century when they were highly prized by the Scottish chieftains.

With the improvement of the sporting rifle in the early nineteenth century, the deerhound breed suffered a setback, as they were no longer needed to stalk deer. The owners of deer forests started to use them less frequently and by the 1830s only a few representatives of the deerhound breed remained. However, they became fashionable again during Queen Victoria's reign and they were used for hunting at both Windsor and Balmoral.

The popularity of stalking deer in the Highlands by man and rifle, without the aid of hounds, increased from the early nineteenth century to the twentieth century. Modern deer stalking predominantly centres on the open slopes of the Scottish Highlands and the red deer is the main quarry, although some roe deer are also stalked. It is estimated there are around 240,000 red deer, and about 40,000 are culled annually. It has become a profitable business for the landowners; the visitor, known as the 'rifle', is usually accompanied by a professional stalker, who selects the particular stag. The stalk may be long and arduous because of the climbing required and the need to traverse several miles around a herd to remain undetected. The deer must never sense the presence of the 'rifle' and the stalker. The deer are found by searching the terrain with a telescope before they are approached with the utmost stealth; the kill is made with a rifle fitted with telescopic sights.

Most visitors are pleased with any prize, but once the most sought-after triumph was a stag possessing a twelve-point set of antlers. This was known as the 'royal' and a stag with such antlers would probably have been about eight years old. Nowadays, a hunter who seeks only to take trophy beasts is considered unsporting. The number of deer culled each year is regulated by the owners of the large estates and steps are taken to control poaching on their land. Severe winters also take their toll of deer.

A Pointer in a Rocky
Landscape (*George
Stubbs*)

5 Game-bird, Wildfowl, Rough and Clay-Pigeon Shooting

The disappearance of the medieval forests, with the resulting decline in the deer population, played a significant role in the popularization of shooting. This occurred after the early sporting guns were first introduced in the latter part of the seventeenth century. The main quarries were the partridge, pheasant, grouse, snipe, woodcock, quail and aquatic wildfowl. Previously, wild birds and fowl were caught by falconry, shooting with the longbow and crossbow, netting and liming. The last, capturing small birds with the use of glutinous bird lime, was much favoured. The lime was smeared on twigs placed in bushes, where the birds were likely to alight and become stuck. Lime strings were also laid out to trap the birds.

The netting of birds relied on the assistance of a setting dog to find the game. At first, probably as early as the thirteenth century, spaniels fulfilled this role, and this led, through the centuries, to the development of the modern setter to indicate game. The dog was trained to take a zigzag path over the countryside until it scented a game-bird or birds under cover. It then immediately halted and raised one of its front legs to signal where the bird was hiding, before settling down on its stomach. It quietly crawled forward until it was close to the quarry then crouched down, completely still. This was known as 'setting'. Two of the hunters then silently attempted to drag a net over both the dog and the bird. Many birds escaped, as great stealth was needed. With the advent of shooting, the role of the setter altered but a dog was still needed to 'point' or indicate the game. Until the mid-nineteenth century, game was always 'walked-up' using pointers and shot 'going away'. Game driven over the guns was introduced later.

When the early muskets were first introduced for shooting game-birds, the quarry was always targeted when on the ground. The flintlock gun came into fashion in about 1600 and lasted until the early 1800s. It relied on a spark from a flint to fire it. The guns often proved dangerous because they misfired frequently and were unreliable when they overheated. In the first half of the seventeenth century, the shooting was usually done from horseback and it was a near impossible task to hit a flying bird. The concept of shooting at a bird on the wing originated in France, but only after improvements in gun design had been made. The fashion spread to England and by the end of the seventeenth century it was considered unsporting to shoot a bird on the ground. This initially applied to grouse and blackcock but later the principle was adopted for the more common pheasants and partridges. The guns available at the time always had a delay between ignition and firing, thus giving the bird a sporting chance of escape.

The early muzzle-loading guns were unwieldy, long and difficult to load with powder, wadding and shot, especially in damp weather. After loading, the charge had to be seated with a ramrod. In addition, there was a pause caused by the need to load between each shot. Improvements in design by the end of the eighteenth century allowed the barrels to be considerably shortened and lightened, with the result that double-barrelled shotguns became more widely used. The double-barrel required reloading after each second shot, thus giving two shots at a fast-moving target, such as a flying bird.

The hazardous problem of misfires with the muzzle-loading shotguns was largely overcome with the invention of the percussion cap during the first decade of the nineteenth century. The precise inventor remains difficult to determine, although a strong claimant must be the Reverend Alexander Forsyth, who obtained a patent in 1807 for the use of mercury fulminate to ignite and fire guns. As a consequence, percussion caps were on sale in England by 1816. They took the form of a copper cap encasing a small charge which, when struck by the gun's hammer, created a flash that passed down the nipple to ignite the powder. This type of muzzle-loading gun utilizing a percussion cap remained in fashion until the next major advance, the invention of the breech-loading or pin-fired gun.

The Frenchman Le Faucheuz patented the idea of a breech-loading shotgun in 1835. It was shown at the Great Exhibition of 1851, held at Crystal Palace in London. This drew the attention of the English sportsmen to its potential and by 1856 it had revolutionized shotgun shooting. It initiated the demise of the cumbersome muzzle-loader, for a cartridge could be used instead of the troublesome powder, wadding and shot. Also, the breech-and-load mechanism enabled shooting to become more accurate, safer and speedier. Joseph Lang was the first British manufacturer of the pinfire breech-loader and Birmingham became the centre of the English gun trade in the nineteenth century. The early ammunition took the form of a cartridge with a protruding pin, which the hammer drove into the cartridge to fire the shot. In 1860, the first centre-fire cartridge was produced by George Daw and the cartridges in use today are still similar in appearance.

Further refinements in gun design took place and by the end of the nineteenth century both hammerless and ejector guns had come onto the market. The double twelve-bore hammerless sidelock ejector gun eventually evolved to monopolize the sporting shooting scene. Some further limited improvements were made but the basic principle remained well-established. Most sportsmen favoured the twelve-bore, although some ladies preferred the sixteen-bore which was lighter. The bore number indicated the size of the gun. The system calculated the number of lead balls of an arbitrary diameter that weighed one pound. If twelve balls weighed one pound, then the diameter of each ball would be 0.747 inches. The twelve-bore shotgun therefore fired shot of this diameter.

The shotguns for game-bird shooting were smooth-bore weapons with a limited range of about 325 yards. The cartridge discharged a cone-shaped pattern of lead shot, with a diameter expanding to between twenty and forty inches. The spread depended on several factors, such as the taper of the barrel, the size of the lead shot and the target range. The spray of shot sometimes succeeded in 'downing' more than one bird at a time.

The shooting of game-birds in England was confined to people of high social status and the large landowners. The development of arable farms with extensive acreage of corn and root crops created ideal conditions for partridges and pheasants to prosper. The lengthy procedure of loading the muzzle-loader before the breech-loader was invented meant that the field method known as 'walking-up' had to be adopted on shoots. In this, the guns or shooters walked in a line over large expanses of open countryside and in front of them they sent their dogs, the pointers or the setters. The dogs would search the terrain until game was scented. They were taught to obey both visual signals and words of command. The pointers were especially noted for their obedience and good nature, the setters equally so for their intelligence and stamina.

Pointers were normally trained to search in pairs, one veering to the right and the other to the left of the terrain. They would turn inwards to meet, before moving apart again to repeat the procedure. This was continued until one of the dogs scented the game. It would then adopt the classic pose of freezing its movement, with the foreleg raised, the head held high and the tail completely still. The nose pointed where the covey was located. The second dog, on seeing the other dog 'point', would also halt and take up a similar stance. The shooter would proceed to the first pointing dog who would slowly move forward to flush the game. Immediately the birds flew, the dog would drop low to the ground in order not to interfere with the shot.

Black Pointer in a
Wooded Landscape
(*J.F. Herring, Sen.*)

Gentleman with
Pointers – Partridge
Shooting
(*J.N. Sartorius*)

A Successful Hit
(*Henry Alken, Sen.*)

Pheasant Shooting
(*William Jones*)

The shot was fairly easy as it was done just after the bird rose and before it could fly at speed. The origin of the modern pointer dog breed in England may date back to the early eighteenth century, when soldiers returned with them after the end of the War of the Spanish Succession.

The setters fulfilled a similar function to the pointers and were also used to locate game. Again, this was done by ranging in a zigzag fashion over wide areas of countryside. Before the advent of the gun they found game and squatted down flat, 'setting', before a net was thrown over both them and the bird. When shooting at flying birds displaced netting, the need to squat and crawl disappeared and dogs were taught to stand up to indicate the position of the game and draw towards it. The modern setter breeds were developed by cross-breeding with the Spanish pointers.

In the early days of shooting with the muzzle-loader, the partridge was the main quarry rather than the pheasant. The hunting of the partridge was considered more genteel and the practice of netting still continued, as well as shooting. By the late eighteenth century, rules and regulations placed the sport of partridge shooting on a more formal basis. A close season was introduced and licences to shoot were required after 1784; the game was the property of the landowner. French partridges, known as 'red legs' because of the distinctive colour of their legs, were imported into England from about 1770 to supplement the native birds, the grey partridges. The French partridges were released in the corn-growing regions of southern and eastern England where they flourished. The patchwork

A Sportsman in his Shooting Gig Driving to the Moors
(*J.F. Herring, Sen.*)

Sportsmen on the
Yorkshire Moors
(J F Herring Sen)

of fields, broken by hedgerows, formed an ideal environment for both types of partridge. The shooting therefore took place over farmland; the birds when flushed from cover flew strongly away and low over the land.

The stocks of partridge in England, especially the native grey, have declined throughout the twentieth century, owing to the cumulative effects of severe winters in the 1940s and 1960s, changed agricultural policies, and the use of weedkillers and pesticides. The early ploughing in of stubble reduced the winter food supply for the birds. The wider usage of toxic agricultural chemicals in cereal fields further reduced the potential food source by destroying insects on which the partridge chicks fed during their first few critical weeks of life. The delicate balance of nature was therefore upset. Many partridge eggs also fell prey to predators, such as the fox and stoat. Stocks of partridge have now begun to increase as some farmers have left untreated stretches of land to encourage wildlife and provide cover. Additionally, partridge chicks are now bred in captivity and released to the wild. The close season for partridge shooting is 2nd February to 31st August but during the season the 'bags' are much diminished compared with former times.

Partridge shooting also declined in the middle of the nineteenth century but for a different reason. The invention of the breech-loading shotgun, with its more rapid rate of fire, allowed a new form of shooting, known as 'driven-shooting', to develop, in addition to the 'walking-up' method. In driven-shooting the guns remained stationary and 'beaters', assisted by dogs in a semicircle, drove the game-birds from the coverts to fly over the guns. Pheasants flew higher and faster than the partridge, with the result that the former offered a greater test of marksmanship to the sportsman. As a result, partridge shooting declined. Driven-shooting did not require the same amount of field craft as was employed in the walking-up method. In the latter, the shooter hunted for his own game; in the driven-shoot the marksman paid others to drive the game to him.

Various types of pheasant had already been introduced into England during the preceding centuries but the huge popularity of driven pheasant shoots demanded the rearing of additional pheasants to satisfy the increased demand. The pheasant replaced the partridge as the most common game-bird. The conservation of the pheasant stocks in the 1850s could only be achieved by the fencing-in of the estates, and the services of gamekeepers were much in demand. Around this time, there were nearly fifteen hundred licensed keepers, and some estates even gave them their own livery to wear. Huge shoots took place and gone were the days when informal shoots were held amongst a few friends. The guns now brought their own men as loaders, and their own dogs, and each individual used two or more shotguns to increase his fire-power. Large estates such as Sandringham evolved, and the size of the 'bags' became important. This was especially relevant in the reign of George V, when thousands of birds would be killed in a royal shoot. House shooting parties became the leading social events on many aristocratic estates.

The planting of extensive coverts was undertaken on the estates at great financial expense. In addition, gamekeepers assisted the survival of the chicks by building covert shelter for the hen pheasants to raise them in relative safety from predators and extremes of weather. Hazel coppices were planted, as well as low shrubs which produced berries as winter food for the birds. The modern practice next developed, involving captive breeding in pens and the release of the hand-reared birds when they were large enough to survive in the wild on their own. Game shooting now depends largely on such specially reared birds.

The heyday of the large shoots for the wealthy lasted until the outbreak of the First World War, in 1914. However, the gigantic cost of maintaining the estates had already become burdensome. A combination of death duties (first introduced in 1898) and income tax depleted the capital available for such pursuits. The result was the even more intensive hand-rearing of pheasants and the formation of shooting syndicates to finance the cost. The pheasant shooting season now ranges from 1st October to 1st February, but birds must not be killed on Sundays or on Christmas Day (this also applies to partridge and grouse). It is estimated that approximately ten per cent of the pheasants reared and released escape the guns to become wild pheasants. However, they do not normally survive in the wild for more than a season or two, as many fall victim to predators.

Another change brought about by the breech-loading gun in the mid-nineteenth century was the decline in the traditional role of the pointer and setter. Dogs were now required for driven-shooting that could 'spring' the game from cover and drive it towards the guns. As many birds were shot, it was also essential to have dogs which could find and retrieve the fallen game. Springer and cocker spaniels played the dual role of flushing game and retrieving it. The specialist retrievers, such as the labradors and the golden retrievers, later came into their own for bringing back wounded and dead game-birds. They were trained to ignore all other birds and distractions. The tracking and recovery of wounded birds was important to the shooting sportsman; they should not be abandoned to suffer and die. Wounded game retrieved would be killed quickly and humanely. The pre-eminence of the labrador among the retriever breeds was established in the early 1900s and the labrador became the most popular gundog for all forms of retrieving. The dogs were assisted in their task by 'pickers-up' stationed behind the line of guns. These men, together with the beaters, were employed by the shoot organizers.

Unlike pheasant and partridge shooting which took place over farmland, the shooting of grouse (the prime target being the red grouse) was always over moorland. The fashion for grouse shooting grew when the railways spread in Victorian times. The rail links gave easier access to the moors of northern England and Scotland. The sportsmen travelled with their guns protected in cases of oak or mahogany, some bound with brass. Unlike pheasants and partridges, grouse could not be bred in captivity and they lived only in the wild, feeding mainly on the young heather of the moor.

The same two established methods were used to shoot grouse. Walking-up was the traditional way, and in the driven-shoot the grouse were driven over the guns in the butts, which were screened by a low turf or stone wall. The latter technique for grouse shooting also started in the second half of the nineteenth century. In both walking-up and driven-shooting, the grouse when 'flushed' rose rapidly and flew swiftly with a low whirring flight. They presented a difficult target and challenge to the shooting sportsman.

Nowadays, grouse shooting has become highly commercialized, with sportsmen paying large sums for shooting rights. Huge areas of moorland in Yorkshire are managed to suit the needs of the grouse. The control of predators assists not only the grouse but benefits all

Shooting in a
Mountain Landscape

Snipe Shooting
(*John Cordrey*)

Spaniels Flushing
Mallards (*George
Armfield*)

Duck Shooting
(*E. Duncan*)

other ground-nesting birds. Systematic burning of large swathes of heather creates the ideal mixture of old and new plants which the red grouse relishes for food and cover. The burning encourages vigorous succulent shoot growth which is essential for the successful rearing of the young birds. As well as the heather, the chicks feed on insects, and a hot summer often results in a decline in the number that are available. Many young birds are then not able to survive. A cold wet spring also results in high chick mortality. Without the commercial demands of the shoot, vast areas of unspoilt moorland would surely have been claimed for other agricultural purposes.

The 'Glorious Twelfth' heralds the opening of the grouse-shooting season; it runs from 12th August to 10th December, but the earlier months are most favoured. As well as the red grouse, the black grouse also resides in northern England and Scotland but its numbers have declined in recent years. Its preferred habitat is on the boundary between moorland and woodland. The male of the species, known generally as the blackcock, is considerably larger than the red grouse. However, the black grouse has never been such a prime target as the red grouse for the shooting sportsman. The other, rarer, species of grouse, the ptarmigan, now only lives at higher altitudes in the Scottish Highlands, and survives well on snow-covered ground. In winter, the whole plumage becomes white but in the summer only the wingtips are white.

The snipe, also valued as a wild bird for the table, offers a difficult target to the marksman. It takes to the air with surprising speed and flies with a swift jerking, zigzag movement. Snipe thrive on freshwater boggy land and flooded fields. Consequently they are found frequently in the Fens of eastern England and in even greater abundance in Ireland and Scotland. Snipe perform a characteristic aerial drumming as they dive. This is done by extending a feather, and is thought to be a procedure to attract a mate. The snipe shooting season runs from 12th August to 31st January.

The other popular wild bird for shooting is the woodcock. Originally a shore bird, it has now taken to the woods. These are migratory birds and are mainly found in Cornwall but much more frequently in southern Ireland. They rely on superb camouflage for protection but when 'flushed' they take an erratic flight amongst the trees and so present a challenging target. The shooting season extends from 1st October to 31st January.

Wildfowl such as the mallard, wigeon and teal constituted an important food source for families through many centuries. This applied especially to those living near marshy areas, such as the Fens of eastern England. In fact, the early draining of the Fens, which began in the seventeenth century, led to considerable conflict because of the loss of wildfowl rights by the local people. Their fierce resistance and the destruction by them of some of the drainage systems installed earned them the name of the 'Fen Tigers'. Before the Fens were drained, undergraduates from Cambridge frequently hunted wildfowl on the uncultivated land in the surrounding vicinity.

Prior to the development of the shotgun, netting of wildfowl was the usual method of capture. The earliest procedure, in use since the thirteenth century, was to drive them into tunnel nets during the moulting season when the young birds were not yet able to fly. This technique caught many hundreds of birds and was especially favoured in the Fens to obtain large supplies for sale to the markets. The practice became so destructive to the wildfowl population that an Act was passed in Parliament in 1534 prohibiting the further use of this method.

Other forms of netting came into service such as the drag, flight and clap nets. With the drag net, men attempted the difficult task of dragging a net over the sleeping quarry. In the case of flight nets, they were suspended vertically in the air by long poles driven into the ground. The effectiveness of the method depended on the skill of the men in anticipating the flight paths of the wildfowl. The third type of net, the clap net, consisted of two nets hinged together and placed on the ground. The fowler, in his concealed hide, would attempt to attract the ducks onto the catching area, before pulling a cord to collapse, or 'clap', the hinged net over the birds. Yet another method of duck catching was to use a baited cage to lure the quarry. When a number of ducks entered, the door was shut by the hunter. These cages were used both on the ground and on floating rafts.

Another widely established method was the decoy. In essence, this enticed wild ducks flying over a pond to land on the water and eventually be persuaded to enter a tall and long wide-mouthed tunnel. The tunnel looked like a transparent circular pipe and was made from a long series of wooden hoops covered with netting. Food thrown onto the water by the decoyman drifted up the mouth of the tunnel. This attracted the live tame ducks, called decoys, to enter it. These belonged to the decoyman who fed them regularly to ensure that they became resident on the pond. The decoys in turn were followed up the tunnel by wild ducks, initially attracted to the pond by the sight of the swimming tame birds. Another method of luring the ducks into the tunnel was to send a small dog, also called a decoy, through it. The decoy dog was trained for the purpose and taught not to bark or frighten the birds. The dog became known as 'the piper' and strangely the wild ducks would follow it, possibly out of sheer curiosity. Whatever the reason, the technique worked.

When sufficient ducks had entered the net tunnel, the decoyman would reveal himself at the entrance to cut off any retreat. The ducks scurried up the tunnel net, which progressively decreased in

A Solitary Marksman

A Retriever with a
Mallard (*J.F. Herring,
Sen.*)

diameter until they reached the end. This was fitted with a
detachable bag in which the ducks were trapped and removed by the
decoyman. Mornings at 11 am and afternoons at 2 pm became the
traditional times to carry out the procedure.

Charles II was intrigued by the method and he had a decoy system
built in St James's Park. Many such decoys were installed on
convenient ponds around England and usually four or five pipes were
used on the same stretch of water. The pond had to be surrounded by
a very wide encircling perimeter of trees and bushes to ensure
complete solitude for the site. Freedom from disturbance was
essential in order to attract the wild ducks. For this reason, when the
shooting of wildfowl came into fashion, it could obviously never be
carried out near a decoy site. During the eighteenth and nineteenth
centuries, catches of several thousand duck in a season were not
uncommon by the decoy method on the east coast of England.

The shooting of wildfowl, both flying wild duck and geese, demanded a considerable amount of expertise in stealth and field craft. The shooting took place mainly on the mudflats below the high-water mark, and good camouflage for the hunter was essential. The shooting method, known as 'flighting', involved the discovery of the favoured line of flight of the wildfowl, to and from their feeding grounds. This knowledge had to be acquired by observation and experience before the hunter could hide in ambush below the anticipated route of the flying birds. The usual periods of day to wait were dawn and dusk. At one time, stalking horses were used to conceal the hunter, before static hides were built by wildfowlers on the marshes.

Artificial wooden decoy ducks were also in fashion to attract birds to fly over the water where the decoys floated. The decoys lured the unsuspecting birds within the range of the hunter's gun. The marksman then attempted to shoot the flying quarry. Later, rubber, metal and, more recently, plastic decoy ducks took the place of wooden ones. Most were manufactured in England but a few were imported from the United States of America during the nineteenth century. Some of the metal decoys were designed to float on wooden bases.

The nineteenth century saw the zenith of the popularity of wildfowling. The men living near coastal regions were the main participants but they were joined by wealthy amateurs who travelled to the coastal marshes for their sporting pastime. They also visited the inland marshes, ponds and lakes in various parts of England to shoot water fowl. The amateurs had to be as hardy as the local men, as wildfowling always took place in winter marshes under damp, cold and extremely miserable conditions. The physical discomfort was unavoidable and the sport was a lonely one too. Bad weather created better sport, as gales brought in more birds seeking shelter. Freezing conditions limited the available area of water for the birds to feed on and so assisted the hunter.

Wildfowling presented high-flying and difficult targets for the marksman. This demanded heavier shotguns than those used for traditional game-bird shooting, with bores ranging from ten to four, and frequently the barrels extended over forty inches. Before the outbreak of the Second World War, heavy swivel guns, with even longer barrels, mounted on punts, came into service for shooting fowl in river estuaries and coastal waters. The weight of the punt-gun dictated that the wildfowl were only shot at when resting on the water in groups or immediately after rising from it. The punt-gunning took place at night as well as in the daytime. Nets and occasionally dogs were used to retrieve the shot birds from the water. Surprisingly, the flintlock used in the earlier days had some advantage over the later breech-loading shotgun. The ignition flash caused stationary or swimming birds to rise and the outspread wings gave a larger target for the expanding shot pattern.

The increase in drainage schemes to reclaim land towards the end of the nineteenth century seriously reduced the areas of natural habitat available for wildfowl, both in inland marshes and in coastal regions. During the twentieth century, many places formerly favoured for wildfowling were converted into sanctuaries and general wildlife reserves. Some offered the wildfowler the privilege of shooting to stabilize the population of the birds. In areas where wildfowling still takes place, far fewer birds are shot than in the past. However, much effort is expended by the wildfowlers to encourage ducks and geese to breed and feed. This is done by improving the areas of open water available and conserving the wet grasslands which the birds enjoy.

Wildfowling clubs play a role in protecting these areas against disturbance and egg collectors. They assist the gamekeepers in this task and help to discourage unauthorized shooting in the area. Irresponsible shooting frequently only wounds birds and the lead shot, deposited in the marshes, poisons other fowl and wildlife. The potential problem of poisoning has been drastically reduced in the United States of America by changing to steel shot.

Despite the large numbers of shooters attracted to the more elite 'walking-up' and 'driven-shoots' and wildfowling, another form of shooting called 'rough-shooting' has always been extremely popular and today it is the main shotgun sport in the United Kingdom. A farmer's permission to shoot over his land is required and the sport is frequently described as 'shooting for the pot'. The shooting is carried out over a relatively small area of land and the participants are normally a small group of friends. They often operate in pairs shooting over their dogs. It therefore remains far less formal than the traditional pheasant and grouse shoots.

The shooters require no 'beaters' to assist them but do need a dog which is capable of performing three tasks: namely locating, flushing and retrieving the quarry. Labradors and springer spaniels perform these three all-round functions admirably. Rough-shooting demands hunting skills as the hunters must search over the land with their dogs for wild game. In the past this may have included partridge, pheasant, snipe, wildfowl and hares. Nowadays, rabbits and woodpigeons predominate and are the most likely bag for the rough-shooter.

In particular, farmers welcome rough-shoots to help cull the woodpigeons on their land. Pigeons cause considerable loss to them by eating newly sown grain and other crops, together with corn when it ripens. Despite shooting which takes place throughout the year,

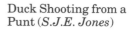
Duck Shooting from a
Punt (*S.J.E. Jones*)

the number of woodpigeons seems to stabilize at a fairly constant
level. Autumn shooting may be responsible for this, as the resulting
reduction in numbers means that there is less competition among
surviving woodpigeons for the available winter food.

When pigeons are the sole quarry, a different technique is required
to achieve a large cull. This demands considerable craft as the birds
are naturally wary, agile and fast flyers. Three main methods are
employed: decoys, 'flighting' and roost shoots. In the first, artificial
decoy pigeons are stood in strategic groups in a field which is a
favourite feeding place of the pigeons. Large numbers of decoys are
needed to imitate a flock of feeding birds and this attracts the wild
pigeons to descend and join them. The shooters, concealed in a hide,
then shoot their quarry with shotguns or sometimes with air-rifles.

The second method, of 'flighting', is similar to that utilized in
wildfowl shooting. The shooters wait in a hide, having first
ascertained the most frequent flight paths taken by the pigeons from
their roosts to their feeding grounds. If the pigeons fly low over the
hide, many shooters favour the use of a twenty-eight-bore shotgun to
scatter shot quickly over a wide area but the twelve-bore, with its
longer range, is preferred when the birds are flying over high and
fast. In the third method, roost shooting, the pigeons are shot after

coming back to roost, using a shotgun or an air-rifle.

Rooks and carrion crows as well as pigeons consume considerable amounts of farmers' food. Culls are therefore frequently carried out and most birds are again killed with shotguns or air-rifles when feeding or returning to roost in the evening. Again, cover is needed by the shooters. In the last century, another weapon, known as a rook rifle, was very occasionally used in addition to the shotgun. The rook rifle fired bullets instead of shot and had a limited range of up to a hundred yards. It was a small-calibre rifle of around ninety-bore. Crows, rooks and pigeons are shot on the ground as well as in the air because the farmers treat them as vermin. This is in contrast to the shooting of game-birds when it is considered unsporting to shoot a bird which is not in flight.

Shooting at live pigeons formed the early origins of the sport of clay-pigeon shooting. In 1780, sportsmen improved their skill at shooting by firing at live pigeons when they were released from under

Sportsmen Retrieving their Quarry
(*S.J.E. Jones*)

Refreshment after a Mixed Bag (*William Jones*)

a hat on the ground. The use of the hat gave the nickname of 'Old Hats' to the participants in this new sport. Live pigeons were also released from baskets and cages at the beginning of the nineteenth century. This led to the development of a trap system, positioned approximately twenty to thirty yards away from the marksmen. The live pigeons were released on command by the pulling of a long cord.

The sport became so popular that several pigeon-shooting centres were opened in London during the early part of the nineteenth century. A series of five traps was set up at the standard distance of thirty yards from the shooters. In annual club events, each marksman was permitted to shoot at twenty live birds each day, on four consecutive days. The sport became so fashionable that country clubs were opened outside the city. Heavy wagering on the results of matches took place. This inevitably led to the shooters using the maximum possible charge in their guns to increase their chance of a hit. Heavy guns, such as ten-bores with barrels approaching thirty-two inches, became favoured. Separate rods were used to load them.

In the 1870s the demand became so great that dummy birds were used in place of live pigeons. The cruelty of shooting live birds, which had been imprisoned, further assisted the change to artificial targets. In the late 1870s, Alexandra, Princess of Wales, expressed her disgust at the shooting of captive live birds. Although this may have eventually helped the practice to be made illegal, it was not finally made so until 1921. The early dummy targets consisted of hollow glass balls filled with feathers. No doubt this was to make a 'hit' by a competitor appear more realistic when the feathers flew, as the glass sphere shattered. The glass balls were thrown into the air by releasing metal springs which were compressed in mechanical traps.

In 1893, the sport was so popular that a need for a governing body became apparent. In response, the Inanimate Bird Shooting Association was formed. Ten years later, in 1903, the word 'clay' was substituted for 'inanimate' and the new body became the Clay Bird Shooting Association. The name was changed again in 1922 to the British Trapshooting Association and yet again in 1928 to the Clay-Pigeon Shooting Association. Most local clubs throughout the country then became affiliated to it.

In clay-pigeon shooting, a saucer-shaped disc is used to simulate a flying bird. The disc is thrown into the air by mechanical means, at a speed approaching 50 mph, from a spring-activated launcher. The shotgun with an effective range of forty yards was always used as the weapon to fire at the target. In competition, the black regulation disc, made of limestone and pitch, had a diameter of 4.29 inches. It disintegrated when hit because of its large spin velocity. Various sizes of shotgun were used initially, but the twelve-bore became the accepted standard weapon.

The spinning clay does not reproduce the erratic flight course taken by a disturbed bird flying away, but variations in launching heights, directions and angles are now used in modern competitions. However, the clay target has a much faster initial acceleration than a live bird and then slows down before dipping towards the ground. Variations in the height of the clay target are achieved by the combination of a high and a low trap-house, positioned 40 yards apart. The competitors stand equidistant from the two trap-houses and many of the targets are 'crossing shots' rather than 'going away' from the shooter. This form of sport, known as skeet shooting, attempts to simulate high- and low-flying birds. The name 'skeet' derives from an ancient Scandinavian word meaning 'to shoot'.

Another form of trap layout, called 'sporting clays', allows an even closer simulation to live birds. For safety reasons, plenty of all-around space is needed and the clay targets are thrown into the air in many different trajectories. Several traps are positioned in various loctions around the competition site and these are 'sprung' without warning to the shooter who carries his gun in the down position. Clay-pigeon shooting thus offers useful practice to marksmen who indulge in other types of shooting.

Two Greyhounds
(*Charles Hancock*)

6 Hare and Rabbit Hunting and Coursing

One of the main differences between hunting and coursing is that in the former the huntsmen and hounds attempt to catch and kill the wild quarry, although it has a good sporting chance to escape; in the latter the main purpose is to test the speed of greyhounds when chasing the wild common brown hare in open countryside. In coursing, very few hares are killed, the vast majority escaping unharmed. Another very important difference is that in the hunting of the hare, harrier and beagle hounds track the quarry by scent but in coursing the pursuit is with greyhounds who chase by sight alone.

When the hunting of the hare is carried out by men on foot, it is known as beagling because beagle hounds are used to follow the scent. If the hare is hunted by mounted horsemen then scent-tracking harrier hounds are used. Beagles are much smaller and slower than harriers and therefore easier to keep up with when following on foot. Beagles stand less than sixteen inches at the shoulder, while harriers stand at a maximum height of twenty-one inches.

In the early part of the seventeenth century, King James I hunted the hare with mounted followers but at first he ignored the essence of the true sporting spirit by bringing live hares in baskets to the heath at Newmarket. These were released for his day's hunting. He became so enthusiastic that he spent much of his time at Newmarket, where the flat open spaces provided excellent terrain for such activities and wild hares were found in abundance, so there was no real reason to use captive hares. The chasing of the hare dominated the scene at Newmarket for many years and later, King Charles II hunted a pack of beagles on the heath. The coursing of hares took place there as well. The popularity of horse racing increased as the seventeenth century progressed and Newmarket then became the headquarters of the turf and the most important venue for the sport.

Wild hares live above ground in well-defined territories of between one and two square miles, and spend the day resting in shallow depressions they dig in the ground. They mostly feed at night. The hollows used for rest and cover are known as 'forms', and one end is deeper than the other to accommodate the hare's large and powerful hindquarters. Hares know their territory intimately and when disturbed they remain absolutely still until the last moment. They then dash away at high speed, usually keeping within their established territory. Flight seems to be a natural instinctive response to danger and fear of attack from predators. The hare's main enemies are farmers with shotguns, foxes, stoats and large birds of prey. When hunted, they twist and double back on their tracks, often sending the pursuers around in circles. The hare relies on its highly sensitive hearing to detect any approaching danger, and when running can reach a speed of 35 mph, moving across the ground with a leapfrog motion. They can jump to a height of more than six feet. Hares are much faster than harriers and beagle hounds, so they always have an excellent chance of eluding them during a hunt. It is often the diseased and older hares that are caught. The leading hound kills the hare by breaking the neck when it brings it down.

Hare hunting offered a supreme test of skill to the English country gentlemen of the seventeenth and eighteenth centuries. With mounted followers, it ranked second only to stag hunting and many preferred it to fox hunting. This was because it presented a greater challenge, as the scent of the hare was less obvious than that of the fox. By the end of the eighteenth century, harrier packs were numerous but only a handful of beagle packs hunted regularly on foot. Sportsmen obviously preferred to ride with hounds rather than walk. This contrasted with Tudor times, when beagling was the more popular with the English gentry before it declined towards the end of the sixteenth century.

One of the oldest harrier packs in England was the Holcombe in Lancashire, which was formed in the seventeenth century, but the stronghold for hare hunting later became East Anglia, and the Cambridgeshire pack was founded in 1745. The preference for hunting hares with harriers and mounted huntsmen continued until the 1850s, although it had started to decrease somewhat after the 1820s. In the 1820s, Parson Honywood from Coggeshall in Essex initiated the resurgence of beagling by breeding a better type of hound to accompany the huntsmen. As a result, by the second part of the nineteenth century, hunting on foot with beagles had gained a wide following. Many packs were formed, especially in Surrey and Sussex. The sport gradually became more organized and The Association of Masters of Harriers and Beagles was founded in 1891. A stud book was also established, with separate sections for harriers and beagles.

During the first half of the twentieth century, beagling became immensely popular and attracted many supporters from a wide spectrum of society; no horse was required to enjoy a day's sport. It was therefore cheap to participate. As well as beagle hounds, packs of basset hounds were used to hunt the hare on foot. The basset is gifted with an exceptional nose which allows it to follow scent with great perseverance. Several basset packs were formed in 1884 and one of the best, the Walhampton, hunted the New Forest up to 1932, when its name changed to The Westerby. At the beginning of the 1990s there were still around ten packs of basset hounds operating in Britain, together with eighty to ninety packs of beagles and about twenty-five packs of harriers. This was despite many mergers of packs in the 1970s, owing to the reduced areas of countryside available to the hunts because of land development and the resulting decrease in the number of hares.

The hare hunting season starts in the autumn and finishes at the end of March. This ensures that the harvest crops are not disturbed and that the hares are allowed to breed without interference from man. All official packs of hounds are registered with The Association of Masters of Harriers and Beagles, which administers the rules of hare hunting, as it has done since 1891. Each pack operates in its own approved registered hunting country. For hare hunting, whether with harriers or beagles, the Master and his hunt staff wear a traditional green and white livery, in contrast to the scarlet or pink of the fox-hunter. The dress generally consists of a green coat, stockings and white breeches. Black caps are usually worn. A very few hunts wear blue coats instead of green. The Master organizes the hunt and his huntsman controls the hounds while out hunting by the use of voice and horn. The Master, his huntsman and the whippers-in, who assist in keeping the hounds together, are greatly outnumbered by the followers of the hunt. In beagling especially, all concerned have to be very fit, as the hunt on foot may progress over several miles owing to doubling back, and various obstacles may have to be climbed.

The rival sport of hare coursing is much older than hunting the hare with harriers and beagles. Coursing took place in the Middle East as long ago as 2000 BC, when 'gazehounds', the forerunner of the greyhound, hunted exclusively by sight rather than scent. The Greek historian, Arrian, described early rules for coursing in the second century AD, and the sport of coursing was established in England long before the Romans came. The Romans continued the sport and loved to test greyhounds in competition when chasing the hare. Arrian, who became a Roman said in AD 116 that 'the sport was to test the speed of the chasing dogs and the true sportsman was glad if the hare escaped'. This sentiment still applies to modern coursing as the objective is to test greyhounds and not to kill hares.

During the reign of Elizabeth I, coursing became fashionable as well as popular throughout England. The Duke of Norfolk drew up the first established rules for the sport at the Queen's request in the sixteenth century and these became known as 'The Laws of the Leash'. However, it was not until the seventeenth century, in Charles I's reign, that coursing trials in public were first held. It was during the next century, in 1776, that the first public coursing club was founded by Lord Orford at Swaffham in Norfolk. Lord Orford was a distinguished breeder of greyhounds and became known as the 'Father of Coursing'. His best dog, named Czarina, won forty-seven matches and remained unbeaten. Strangely, the club when first formed was limited to twenty-six members only, the exact number of letters in the alphabet. Each member had to start the name of his dog with a particular letter of the alphabet. It was therefore only possible for a new member to join when an existing member retired or died. The Swaffham Club still thrives.

Greyhounds 'Spot', 'Skylark', 'Nettle' and 'Sky' (*J.F. Herring, Sen.*)

The formation of the Swaffham Club quickly led to the birth of several others. In these early days, gentlemen normally went coursing on horseback. The Ashdown Park Club came into being in 1780 and the Newmarket Coursing Society in 1805. The latter changed its name later to the South of England Club. Clubs and meetings were arranged in all parts of the country where hares thrived and the terrain was flat, open and suitable for coursing. Many coursing meetings took place in the countryside around Louth in Lincolnshire during the late eighteenth century, and in the early nineteenth century meetings were organized at Flixton in Yorkshire, and Bothal in Northumberland. Wiltshire became well known for its prestigious coursing club at Amesbury near Stonehenge on Salisbury Plain during the late eighteenth century. Perhaps the most famous club, the Altcar Club in Lancashire, was founded in 1825 by Lord Molyneux. Many industrialists enjoyed the sport and it became extremely popular throughout Lancashire. The flat areas of Cheshire were also used for coursing.

The early days of coursing greyhounds saw annual matches arranged between the Swaffham Club and the Amesbury Club during the 1780s. In addition, the South of England Club organized events in Cambridgeshire, Wiltshire and Hampshire. Participants

Hounds in Leash
(*Richard Jones*)

competed for cups and prestige; the main trophies were the South of England Cup and the Barbican Cup. In 1836 the Waterloo Cup, the classic event of coursing, was run for the first time at Altcar, near Liverpool. As the popularity of the sport grew, it was decided that the early rules drafted by the Duke of Norfolk should be updated. In 1834, a new standard set was compiled by Thacker and issued in the *Courser's Companion*. Thacker also published, from 1842 to 1858, the *Courser's Annual Remembrance*, which recorded the results from the various coursing meetings, together with some details of the breeding of the greyhounds.

In 1858, the National Coursing Club was formed by a combination of landowners and businessmen and it became the official governing body of the sport. The Club based its rules on Thacker's, and accepted his *Courser's Annual Remembrance* as the coursing calendar. In its

Going Out (*Samuel Alken*)

early days, the National Coursing Club mainly regulated the competitions between the aristocratic clubs, such as the Swaffham and the Altcar. In 1864, it officiated over a large coursing competition at Stonehenge involving dozens of greyhounds. This took place over seven days and was advertised as 'The Altcar Club' against 'The World'. The Altcar Club won the event. The popularity of coursing grew and by 1873 there were 169 coursing clubs established in the United Kingdom. This necessitated a decree by the National Coursing Club that all greyhounds taking part in coursing under its jurisdiction must be registered. The date set for this was 15th July 1883. Registration followed naturally from the National Coursing Club's inauguration of the Greyhound Stud Book in the previous year, and it has administered registration ever since. The establishment of the Stud Book triggered enormous investments in the perfection of the breed to optimize speed and courage.

Prestigious events, such as the Waterloo Cup, started to attract vast numbers of spectators in the Victorian era because of the coming of the railways. Daily crowds of seventy-five thousand flocked to the Waterloo Cup. However, in 1926 the arrival of track greyhound racing from America, with an artificial hare, brought an astonishing popularity in the new sport during the following years. The first meeting was held at Manchester and by 1932 the total attendance at

Greyhounds Coursing a Hare (*J.F. Sartorius*)

Mounted Gentleman
Observing Course
(*J.N. Sartorius*)

Two Gentlemen with
Coursing Greyhounds
(*J.N. Sartorius*)

A Coursing Meeting
(*T. Bretland*)

all the tracks in the United Kingdom was 20 million. This inevitably led to a decline in attendances at coursing meetings. Despite this, thirty-nine thousand people still watched the Waterloo Cup in 1939 and even today around ten thousand people attend the three-day coursing meeting. The event is held in February on Lord Sefton's Estate at Altcar. The Waterloo Cup was originally the brain-child of William Lynn, the proprietor of the old Waterloo Hotel in Liverpool. He first ran the meeting as an extra event to the steeplechase at Aintree, which later became known as 'The Grand National'. For the first running in 1836 of the Waterloo Cup the competition was restricted to eight greyhounds but by 1839 the entries had increased to thirty-two. In 1858 the number was sixty-four, and by this time the Waterloo Cup had earned worldwide acclaim.

Famous coursing greyhounds became national heroes. Two of the most famous were born in 1866: 'Bab at the Bowster', and 'Master McGrath'. The former won sixty-two out of her sixty-seven courses, whilst the latter, owned by Lord Lurgan, was the first greyhound to win the Waterloo Cup three times, in 1868, 1869 and 1870. Queen Victoria gave 'Master McGrath' and his trainer a royal audience at

Windsor Castle after the remarkable achievement. Another famous greyhound was soon to follow. This was 'Fullerton', born in 1887, and he was awarded the Waterloo Cup from 1890 to 1892. He won thirty-one out of thirty-three courses. When the results of the Cup were released, carrier pigeons carried the news to all the major cities in Britain, and the Stock Exchange closed early to study the results. Despite their successes in winning the Waterloo Cup, several winners did not kill a single hare in their series of courses.

Modern coursing always takes place in open country and the wild brown hares are only chased when at liberty on their own familiar territory. Hares are never released for coursing. The hare is pursued by a pair of greyhounds and the rules of coursing are designed specifically to help the hare escape. There are two types of coursing, 'walked-up' and 'driven'. In the former, as in rough-shooting, the participants walk in a line across the flat expanse of grass to be coursed over until a hare is disturbed. Usually in the centre of the line is the 'slipper', who has a pair of greyhounds on a slip leash which enables him to release them both quickly and simultaneously. The skill of the 'slipper' plays a very important role in the course. He is a trained official licensed by the National Coursing Club. The two competing greyhounds are never released until the hare has a start of at least eighty yards and has a good chance of escape. It is not permitted to restrict the hare's running in any way. The start to the hare is given because the greyhound has an initial speed advantage over the quarry but this is usually negated by the greater stamina of the hare after the hound has run the eighty-yard slip.

In the alternative type of coursing, 'the driven', beaters drive the hares one by one onto the running grounds, past the 'slipper' who is under cover in a 'hide', also known as a 'shy' or 'hurdle'. The slipper again will not release the two competing greyhounds until the hare is at least eighty yards in front. A mounted umpire judges the coursing and takes a position about a hundred yards ahead of the slipper. The umpire traditionally wears a scarlet hunting coat for the main purpose of being conspicuous to all. He needs a horse to enable him to keep up with and observe the coursing as it progresses.

Each greyhound wears a distinguishing red or white collar. The umpire awards points to each hound for its speed, its ability to overtake the other dog (known as a 'go-by') and for forcing the hare to turn sharply at right-angles to evade its pursuers. A hare weighing 10 to 12 lb can turn very quickly within its own length, whilst the much heavier greyhound will always overshoot and is slow to change direction. The kill, if it happens, is not significant to the scoring, as most hares escape. In fact, contrary to popular belief, about ninety per cent of hares make good their escape. As the greyhounds chase by sight, once the hare has disappeared they pull up. When an individual course is completed, the umpire raises a white or red flag to indicate the winning greyhound. An average course lasts just thirty-five to forty seconds, in which time a greyhound can cover a third of a mile.

After the umpire signals the winning dog, the slipper prepares for the next course. The competition runs as a simple knockout, the winner of the first course meeting the winner of the second, and so on. The winners progress through each round until the final is held between the two remaining greyhounds. The stakes are run over one, two or three days. In the prestigious sixty-four-runner Waterloo Cup a greyhound will run six times over the three-day meeting. In such an event, special refuges called 'soughs' are installed to assist the hare's escape.

During the 1880s, a different form of coursing called 'park coursing' gained popularity. Hares were released from a box on an artificial enclosed course; however, this has been prohibited in England since 1914, and is contrary to National Coursing Club rules. It was not regarded as fair and sporting. In its heyday, though, several companies purchased large estates like Kempton, Haydock and Gosforth (Newcastle) Parks to run such events. Eventually, when attendances declined owing to the lack of betting interest as so many dogs started at very short odds, the courses were converted into the now famous horse racetracks.

Until the outbreak of the First World War in 1914, most greyhounds for coursing were kept and trained in large private kennels, housing fifty to a hundred dogs. Many of these kennels declined during the war years and after 1918 small kennels housing just a few greyhounds became more usual. There has never been a statute stipulating a close season for coursing but the National Coursing Club bans the sport between 11th March and 14th September, so that the hares are undisturbed during the breeding season. In general, the number of hares on farmland has decreased, especially in areas where farmers spray with pesticides. Additionally, shooting has considerably reduced hare populations as farmers consider them pests, because they eat growing corn and other crops. In order to preserve hares, chemical sprays are not used on estates, such as Altcar, where coursing takes place. Game conservancy research has shown that hare numbers are increasing in these areas, against the national trend.

In 1976, a House of Lords Select Committee was commissioned to report on the sport of coursing. The Committee concluded that the amount of cruelty in coursing was less than one per cent of that caused by shooting the hare. It added that the ethical question should be left to the individual conscience, and parliamentary legislation was not necessary. Many attempts have since been made

The Kill (*Samuel Alken*)

to make coursing illegal, as opponents claim that the hares are terrified during the chase and they condemn the sport as extremely cruel. Paradoxically, they admit that the sport ensures the preservation of the hare and that few are killed. The Royal Society for the Prevention of Cruelty to Animals opposes the sport. In 1993, there were still more than twenty greyhound coursing clubs affiliated to the National Coursing Club.

Unfortunately, during the 1990s unofficial hare coursing meets have been held surreptitiously in the traditional hare coursing country south of Newmarket. This area was probably selected because it is flat, isolated and close to the M11 and London. Local farmers suggest an additional reason: the land set aside under EC agricultural policies has encouraged hares to thrive. It is thought that many of the gangs who take part come from London and they bring with them their lurchers in order to gamble. They descend on private land without permission and give the sport of coursing an appallingly cruel reputation as many hares are killed. The police state that the main problem for them is that only the civil law of trespass is being broken, which normally results in a small fine. However, if a dead hare is taken off private land the offence becomes one of poaching.

In areas such as East Anglia where hares are more abundant, farmers have reported large gatherings of hares on moonlit nights. These 'hare parliaments', as they are commonly called, involve up to twenty hares sitting motionless in a circle. Hares have been known to move to the centre of the circle and box each other like kangaroos, by rising on their hind legs, in front of the assembled parliament. This strange behaviour usually occurs during the mating season, around March and April, and it has led to several common expressions such as 'the madness of the March hare' or 'mad as a March hare'.

Although hares are nearly always found in open farmland, they are also occasionally discovered amongst sand dunes and in woodland. The use of wooded areas by hares increased significantly after the myxomatosis in the early 1950s which annihilated nearly 60 million of the rabbit population. This inevitably led to a decline in the number of predators, such as buzzards, because of the loss of a food source. The hares occupied the former terrain of the rabbits and an evolutionary territory change took place, as hares normally never mix with rabbits. Rabbits are now less prone to myxomatosis and their numbers have increased. No doubt most of their former lost territory has been reclaimed from the hares, whose numbers have fallen during the last few decades.

When hares were more plentiful, it was customary to arrange large hare shoots and these took place after the game-bird season closed, although legally hares could be killed at any time on private fenced land. Beaters and dogs drove the hares into the range of the guns. On moorland and unfenced cultivated land there was a close season for killing hares from 1st April to 10th December in England and Wales, from 1st April to 30th June in Scotland, and from 1st February to 11th August in Northern Ireland. To deter the poacher, hares could not be killed at night except by a landowner on his own property. The close seasons still apply.

The Normans originally introduced rabbits to England from France during the twelfth century, as a source of food and fur. They encouraged the rabbits to breed in artificial warrens, or 'coning-earths', often in sheep-rearing areas and regions where the soil was sandy. The coning-earths mainly consisted of small mounds constructed in an enclosure where they could be easily farmed. The warrens were protected against poachers by a ditch, together with a surrounding hedge or fence. In those days, rabbit meat was considered a delicacy but by the fourteenth century rabbits had become a plague in England. They were hunted by farmers not only for food but as pests, and much later, in the nineteenth century, whippets were used to course them. The whippet breed of dog was developed in England for this purpose around 1850 by crossing terriers, such as Manchester terriers and Bedlington terriers, with small greyhounds.

The sport of coursing rabbits with competing whippets gained it the reputation of being the poor man's hare coursing substitute. The whippet was identified as a 'poor man's greyhound'. The dog became a firm favourite with the miners and working-class people in the north of England. Lancashire became the home of whippet coursing. The whippets could cover two hundred yards in about twelve seconds. Unlike hare coursing, the rabbits could not be driven across fields as they would dart into their burrows. They had to be netted in advance for coursing and quickly transported to the track so that they were still fresh and active.

Many of the so-called enclosed tracks were constructed at the back of public houses for the coursing. Landlords encouraged the sport to attract extra customers to drink, as most pubs stayed open all day before the outbreak of the First World War. Heavy bets were often struck before each course. In the coursing, the rabbit was held by the loose skin at the back of its neck and placed on a sawdust spot about 60 yards in front of the two competing whippets. The dogs were then 'slipped' and again the skill of the slipper was extremely important. Each dog wore a different-coloured ribbon around its neck and the judge wore a similar one on each arm. After the course, he raised the arm with the winning dog's colour to inform the spectators of the result. In most cases, it was the dog that caught and killed the rabbit. The rabbit was probably terrified by the noise and the strange surroundings and often did not run when it was released. Even if it ran, there was little chance of escape on an enclosed track.

Dogs were matched either by a random draw or by selecting two dogs known to be of similar ability from a study of their previous form. The competition was on a knockout basis and each winner was matched again until the winning dog emerged. There may have been sixty-two courses to decide the winner, so the whippets had to have stamina as well as speed. The charm of whippet coursing to the working-class man was that he could feed, train and take pride in his own dog, rather than use a recognized trainer to do the job for him, which is what happened later in track greyhound racing.

After enclosed live rabbit coursing meetings were stopped at the end of the First World War, the chasing of an artificial lure was substituted. Amateur whippet racing without a live rabbit was the forerunner in England of the highly professional and organized greyhound racing which was to become so popular later. Whippet racing then declined in popularity, although there are still some organized meetings in England today.

Unlike the sport of coursing, the hunting of rabbits for food by farmers and poachers has spanned many centuries. The ferret has been an ally to all in their hunting techniques (see Chapter 10). The exact origin of the ferret, a domesticated form of polecat, remains obscure. The Romans may have first introduced them into England to destroy rats and other vermin but it is more likely that they were brought over from the continent in the twelfth century.

The shooting of rabbits relies on two main methods to flush them into the open: ferreting and laying-out. In the first method, the ferret is sent down the burrow and hunts for the rabbits by scent and sound. The ferret is muzzled to prevent it killing the rabbits. It drives the rabbits from the warren and they are then shot as they bolt. The rabbits when bolting achieve top speed quickly and therefore they provide a good test of marksmanship. Some farmers prefer to net the rabbits as they hurtle out of the burrows. However, netting can hardly be classified as a sport, although it is a part of hunting history.

The alternative method of hunting rabbits, known as laying-out, does not involve the use of a ferret. Instead a gamekeeper waits until

Coursing on Ascot
Heath (*E. Bristow*)

the rabbits leave their burrows to feed at dusk. He then goes around the burrows and sprinkles a foul-smelling mixture, usually based on an unrefined kerosene, in each rabbit-hole entrance. When they return from feeding the rabbits do not enter their burrows because of the smell. Instead, they lay-out under cover of bushes and undergrowth. The following day beaters and spaniels are used to disturb them and they are shot as they run in the open.

Another hunting method employed by countrymen, particularly before the shotgun became popular, was rabbit catching with long nets. This was best done on a dark night when the wind was blowing to mask the sound of the rabbit catcher. Preferably, the wind blew in the direction of the burrows after the rabbits had left them to feed. It was even better if it was raining slightly as the rabbits wandered further afield. The rabbit catcher remained as quiet as possible and never talked to his assistant. A long loose net, which could range from fifty to two hundred yards in length, was then suspended vertically on sticks in front of the burrows by the hedge or bank. The nets were tan in colour so that they could not be seen by the rabbits in the dark. The vertical net was three to five feet high and it was left with plenty of slack between the supporting sticks, so that it assumed the appearance of a series of large joined bags. The sticks were placed about ten yards apart in the ground. When the rabbits later bolted back to their burrows they became entangled in the loose netting. The trapped rabbits were then killed quickly and silently by the two rabbit catchers, usually by dislocating their necks.

Two methods were used to net the rabbits. The first allowed a dog to range over the complete field backwards and forwards in order to drive them towards the net. A good dog was trained not to try to catch the rabbits as they ran or touch them when they became entangled in the net. The sole duty of the dog was to make the rabbits bolt into the long net.

The second method, known as 'lining-in', only needed two men. They crept silently along the side of the field to reach the opposite end from the netting which they had put up. They then quietly unrolled a long line of twine right across the length of the field and drew it tight, each man holding one end. The line was kept taut and parallel to the long net at the opposite end of the field. The men then walked towards the net, one walking along each side of the field. As they walked with the strained line they jerked it at intervals and any unsuspecting feeding rabbit which was touched bolted at once towards the waiting net. The whole field was silently walked across until the net was reached and the entangled rabbits were despatched by the men. Although rabbits could be killed at any time of the year, this technique could only be used legally at night, on the farmer's own land. This, as in the case of hares, was to prevent unauthorized poaching.

In modern times, many rabbits are shot using the technique known as 'lamping'. This became possible with the development of the high-intensity quartz halogen lamp which emits an intense light beam. The lamp is available in a portable form and therefore can be carried, or mounted on a small truck. If carried by hand, one man holds and directs the lamp and his companion does the shooting. When switched on at night, the light dazzles and transfixes for a few moments any rabbits caught in its beam. They are shot, as also are any foxes which may be spotted. As with netting, lamping cannot be classified as a sport but highlights a modern step in hunting history.

Standing Jump
(*J.N. Sartorius*)

7 Fox-hunting

Many people preferred the exciting chase after the fox when this alternative sport started to gain popularity during the eighteenth century. However, hare hunting had always attracted ardent followers and the change was very slow. The number of harrier packs pursuing the hare exceeded that of foxhounds chasing the fox until about the 1830s. Eventually, fox-hunting gained a huge following and it became an established tradition of the English countryside.

Before the eighteenth century, foxes were treated purely as vermin and not hunted with any sporting spirit; for example, as early as the thirteenth century they were dug out of their earths, netted and killed. At this time, Edward I gave permission to some of the abbots to hunt foxes in the Royal Forests to control their numbers. In the fifteenth and sixteenth centuries, the fox continued to be treated as vermin. After digging out from its earth, the fox was sometimes bagged and baited with dogs, before finally being destroyed. An early attempt to hunt the fox with hounds was made in Norfolk in 1534, and many others followed. The scent of the fox was strong and easier to follow than that of the hare and it was slowly followed until the hounds tracked it back to the fox's earth. The fox was then dug out, killed and given to the hounds. In these days, foxes were still not chased in the open for sport. Most of the hunts in the sixteenth century took place between January and March when the stag was not hunted. Many of the nobility and gentry thought it below their high estate to hunt vermin, such as the fox, with hounds for sport.

It was the farmers in the north of England who realized first that the fox was perhaps the most intelligent and cunning of all the beasts of the chase, nearly a hundred years before their more southern counterparts. Therefore, the early beginnings of modern fox-hunting as a sport started in the north during the seventeenth century and later spread down to the south of England. Modern fox-hunting means the hunting of the fox in its wild and natural state in the open with a pack of hounds. The Bilsdale in Yorkshire has claims to be one of the oldest fox-hunts in England. Although predominantly a farmers' hunt, having had several farmers as Masters during its history, it was recorded that the Duke of Buckingham hunted foxes in the area during 1670.

One of the earliest Midlands packs of hounds was founded by Squire Thomas Boothby in 1698. This was kept exclusively to hunt the fox in the countryside around Quorn in Leicestershire. This later led to Hugo Meynell establishing the reputation of the Quorn as the most famous pack of foxhounds in England during the second half of the eighteenth century. He went to live in Quordon Hall, near Loughborough, in 1753. Another early Midlands pack was the Cottesmore which was also based in Leicestershire and Rutland during the latter part of the seventeenth century, becoming extremely well known in the eighteenth century. Other eighteenth-century packs which were later to become famous in the Leicestershire area were the Belvoir and the Fernie. The Belvoir was originally the family pack of the Dukes of Rutland and although based in Leicestershire actually met in Lincolnshire. The Fernie hunted exclusively in Leicestershire. Another old-established pack was the Pytchley, founded in the 1770s, again in the Midlands. From around 1850, the five hunting countries of the Quorn, Cottesmore, Belvoir, Fernie and Pytchley became known as 'The Shires'.

Many other notable packs of foxhounds were formed during the late seventeenth and eighteenth centuries, such as the Beaufort, Fitzwilliam, Heythrop, Berkeley, Grafton and Charlton. William III, Queen Anne, George I and George II all hunted at various times with the Charlton in Sussex. The hunt was originally founded in the 1670s by a supporter of the Duke of Monmouth at the village of Charlton. It became the most famous and fashionable in the country but was disbanded in 1815. Its most famous run took place on 26th January 1738, when a fox was located in East Dean Wood at 8.15 am and the hounds ran all day until 5.50 pm. During the hunt the Duke of Richmond used five horses, having lamed three.

During the eighteenth century, London was still comparatively rural and the Berkeley hounds hunted as far as Kensington Gardens. Most of the early packs were owned and run by individuals of the aristocracy and were hunted as private family packs. For example, the Duke of Beaufort's originally hunted stags but changed to fox-hunting in the late eighteenth century. Its extensive hunting territory covered parts of Gloucestershire, Somerset and Wiltshire. Later, the Beaufort Hunt was to gain a prestigious reputation for the foxhounds it bred, and the blood lines developed were used to benefit other packs in England.

During the first half of the eighteenth century, the mounted riders following the hounds had very few fences and obstacles to hinder their progress. When they came to an occasional barrier which caused them to halt, they would dismount and lead their horses around it. When a hedge was encountered that was difficult to negotiate, the rider often dismounted to grasp his mount's tail and allowed the horse to drag him through it. If an attempt was made to jump an obstacle it was always taken from a standing position. The hounds used at the time were relatively slow and they varied considerably in size. They were allowed to hunt at their own pace, without interference from the huntsman. The whole hunting procedure therefore progressed slowly, as most of the horses were heavy and lacked speed. Many meets took place at sunrise, as it was thought that foxes ran more slowly in the early morning. It became fashionable at this time, around 1740, to make the horse's tail look decorative in the shape of a fan. This was done by cruelly cutting into the muscle in the horse's dock to make the tail hairs stand up. The horse's ears were often mutilated as well, by cropping them.

Despite the leisurely pace of the chase, there were inevitable stragglers who did not witness the end of a successful hunt. This led to the start of the custom known as 'capping' in the mid-eighteenth century. This involved the hanging-up of the dead fox in a tree, under the pretence that it excited the hounds and improved their future keenness. A more likely reason was that it gave a hunt servant time to pass his cap around to collect a tip for the huntsman, from each follower of the hunt. The dead fox was left in the tree until the last stragglers arrived, and they could not escape contributing to the cap too.

The leisurely pace of fox-hunting was to change dramatically in the reign of George III, during the period of the 1760s to the 1790s, when the enclosure of land for farming purposes came into wide practice. Men cleared ancient woodlands to create land for large improved grassland farming, where stock could be safely grazed. This resulted in the erection of fences and the laying of hedges to keep the stock enclosed in the fields. A variety of different types of fence were used for the purpose, such as posts and rails, oxers and double oxers. An oxer was a laid hedge with a ditch on one or both sides, with an oak rail to protect it. The purpose of the rail was to prevent bullocks, worried by summer flies, crashing into the hedge when it was still immature. The hedge was laid by cutting halfway through the sturdiest stems and branches and bending them from vertical positions into horizontal ones. They were then usually tied into place. The partially severed stems and branches soon grew to produce a dense stock-proof hedge.

The thick, wide hedge not only offered a good test of courage for horse and rider when jumping during the hunt but also gave cover to foxes. Other coverts were also provided especially for the foxes, by the planting of small woods of ash and oak, together with copses and clumps of bushes at strategic positions. Eventually, during the hunt

Mr. Osbaldeston riding 'Tranby' in his 'Race Against Time' (*J.F. Herring, Sen.*)

a fox was driven from covert to covert. Another advantage of the new system of farming was that the open grass fields, enclosed by hedges, were ideal to retain the scent left by the fox.

The Industrial Revolution, which started during the second half of the eighteenth century, created a less populated countryside, with many people moving to work in the towns from their former cottage industries. This assisted the growing popularity of fox-hunting as riders could travel more safely at speed along tracks and over fields. The resulting combination of the hedges, fences, coverts, large grass fields and fewer people offered ideal conditions for fox-hunting. Leicestershire and Rutland in particular had large areas of enclosed grazing land. As a consequence, Melton Mowbray in Leicestershire became the mecca of the fox-hunting world by the early nineteenth century. It attracted many wealthy riders from outside the region who could afford several horses, to hunt five or six days a week. The growing popularity of fox-hunting encouraged many gentry to stay in the countryside, rather than spending their time in London or visiting the spa towns to take the waters. Many joined the hunt to ride fast and be able to jump over obstacles at speed. It was a new, exhilarating experience for them.

The increased pace of the hunt demanded a new technique of hunting, with the use of faster horses and better hounds. Many of the horses were at first badly treated and ridden to exhaustion; runs up to ten miles were fairly frequent. Lord Sefton introduced the concept of switching to a reserve fresh horse during the course of the hunt. This was initiated during his Mastership of the Quorn during 1800 to 1802. In addition, the need for both speed and stamina focused the fox-hunters' attention on improving the breeding of their horses. Thoroughbred horses were imported into England and in the early nineteenth century, hunter-class animals were bred with thoroughbred blood to achieve the desired combination of speed and stamina. A further requirement was the ability to jump fences safely and boldly on different types of 'going'. Around 1815, a new fashion started of clipping horses to remove their winter coat, although their legs were left unclipped to provide protection against thorns and knocks. The thoroughbred blood also triggered the urgent need for the rider to have better control of his mount and this saw a wider use of the running martingale as part of the horses' tack. This device had been introduced in the late eighteenth century and restricted the ability of the horse to raise its head high to avoid the bit and therefore evade the rider's control. By the middle of the nineteenth century, double bridles also became fashionable to assist the rider during hunting. Many other experiments were made using various bits and bridles for the hunting field. In contrast, the snaffle bit used in horse racing has remained relatively unchanged during its history.

As well as the horses, the hounds needed to possess speed and stamina but with the extra requirement of a good scenting nose. They had to be able to keep ahead of the horses. Also, a fit fox could run much faster than a foxhound and travel quickly over long distances. It was imperative for the hounds to keep reasonably close behind; otherwise the scent grew cold. It was essential as well for the hounds to follow only the scent of the fox and to disregard distractions, such as the scent of a hare or deer. It was also important for the hounds to be controlled and well behaved. These various requirements gradually brought improvements in the breed of foxhounds during the period 1750 to 1830.

One of the first to realize the importance of the breeding of the foxhound was Hugo Meynell who, as mentioned earlier, assumed the Mastership of the Quorn Hunt after his grandfather, Thomas Boothby. In the second half of the eighteenth century, Hugo Meynell bred hounds for strong running and 'nose', by crossing hounds from the north of England with selected southern ones. Although he bred for the speed and drive required by the Midland hunts, he appreciated that it was futile to produce a hound which could run much faster than its scenting ability. He developed a tactical technique which allowed the hounds to find and follow the scent at their fastest pace without undue interference or shouting from the huntsman. The method was quietly to control the hounds, and the hunt actually took place at a pace dictated by the hounds. Hugo Meynell became known as the 'Father of Fox-hunting', owing to his achievements in both tactics and foxhound breeding. A significant change in tactics occurred when a Mr William Childe (nicknamed 'Flying Childe') came to live in Leicestershire in 1780. He increased the pace of the hunt and rode nearly on top of the hounds, flying over the fences at speed. The excitement given to riders by the fast gallop attracted many to take up fox-hunting. The fine reputation of the Quorn continued and was further enhanced by Tom Firr a century later, when he became huntsman there in 1872. He developed the method known as the 'galloping cast' to assist the hounds to recover a lost scent. This involved sending the hounds out in a wide circle to a place he estimated the fox may have run. This often resulted in the scent being picked-up quickly and the momentum of the chase maintained.

During the second half of the eighteenth century, in various parts of England, other early exponents of fox-hunting were at work. Two of the most notable were Squire Farquharson in the West Country, who hunted from two different kennels in Dorset, and Peter Beckford in Cranborne Chase, straddling the Dorset/Wiltshire border. Peter Beckford wrote a textbook in 1781 entitled *Thoughts on Hunting*, which expounded the techniques and principles of fox-hunting. He philosophized: 'Fox-hunting is now become the sport of gentlemen; nor need any gentleman be ashamed of it'. In a similar fashion to Hugo Meynell, both Farquharson and Beckford insisted that the hounds be allowed to hunt quietly at their own pace and be given plenty of room to do so, in contrast to 'Flying Childe's' racing method.

The Regency squire George Osbaldeston became Master of the Quorn, and he carried on the work of improving the hunting and breeding of hounds. He did this with exceptional skill despite his reputation for high living and being a compulsive gambler. He lost many fortunes during his lifetime and died in poverty in 1865. He once won a bet of a thousand guineas in 1831 by riding two hundred miles in eight hours and forty-two minutes. He used twenty-eight different horses.

In October 1993, the Animal Health Trust at Newmarket arranged an attempt to challenge Osbaldeston's 'Race Against Time'. The stables at Newmarket provided a series of forty-eight different mounts for the rider, who was Peter Scudamore, the recently retired champion National Hunt jockey. His attempt on the record was successful, beating the previous record by four minutes.

Squire George Osbaldeston was not alone in his reputation for high-living and gambling. Many other hunting squires of the eighteenth century acquired a rakish reputation for heavy drinking and playing games of chance. The majority of their time outside of these activities was spent hunting, fishing and shooting. Some reputedly slept with their riding boots on. This applied as well to many of the hunting parsons in the eighteenth century and the beginning of the nineteenth century, who divided their time between hunting, the brandy bottle and the pulpit. Some rode six days a week to hounds and condescended to give a short sermon on the Sabbath.

The Reverend John Russell (more familiarly known as 'Jack Russell' and 'Parson Jack') from the thatched village of Iddesleigh, in Devon, was a notorious Victorian country cleric with a passion for hunting. He died in 1883 at the age of eighty-seven. On many occasions, his cassock disguised the breeches and hunting boots he wore underneath whilst preaching in the pulpit. The Jack Russell terrier was named after him and his terriers used to run with the hounds and were longer legged than the current breed. A

Huntsmen Regaling
(*Samuel Raven*)

contemporary of Parson Jack was the Reverend John Froude from nearby Knowstone on Exmoor. He hunted three days a week and shot on the other four. Many stories have been told of his exploits. One relates that his Bishop was dubious about his behaviour and visited him to give a reprimand. On arrival he was informed by the housekeeper that the Reverend Froude was in bed with a highly contagious fever (probably scarlet fever). The Bishop hurriedly departed on hearing the news and the Reverend Froude jumped out of bed and went out hunting with his friends, who also possessed a fever for 'scarlet' or 'hunting pink'!

There were a host of other parsons who indulged in hunting. The Reverend John Loder formed a foxhound pack in North Berkshire around 1760. The Reverend Billy Butler in the eighteenth century even refused to marry 'the labouring classes' on all hunting days. Even on non-hunting days he insisted on the ceremony being performed very early in the morning to 'keep them on their toes'. The Reverend Griff Lloyd adopted a similar attitude in Oxfordshire during the 1820s; he only performed marriages and burials outside the hunt meeting dates. The first two Masters of the Old Berkshire hunt were clergy, and the Reverend Ellis St John hunted South Berkshire until 1817.

Many of the early hunting parsons were the youngest sons of rich landed families and could well afford the expense of hunting. Several others managed to marry rich heiresses, so they too could indulge in the sport. The Reverend Symmonds hunted in Herefordshire, while the Reverend George Talbot was a Master of a pack hunting in Derbyshire and Staffordshire during the nineteenth century. The list of sporting clergymen who excelled in the hunting field appears endless. Little is recorded about their performance in the pulpit. One is reputed to have defined heaven as 'that beautiful grassy country where there's always a scent and never a blank day'.

The Reverend W. Phillips formed a pack of foxhounds in Cattistock, Dorset, and the Cattistock Hunt, known as the 'True Blue Hunt', was founded in the mid-eighteenth century. However, as the nineteenth century progressed, parsons who went hunting became fewer owing to the disapproval of their superiors and their congregations. Many also came from poorer families and could not afford the expense. By the end of the century, it was fairly rare to discover a hunting parson. The longest surviving sporting clerics were found in the West Country and the fells of the Lake District. The Reverend Edgar Milne was Master of the Cattistock Foxhounds in Dorset from 1900 to 1931, having previously been the Master of the North Buckinghamshire Harriers from 1895 to 1900.

Sheep farming was always a key industry in the Lake District and the fell packs became the most important method of fox control. The fells produced perhaps the most famous name ever associated with fox-hunting, that of John Peel. The name was immortalized purely by its inclusion in the words of a popular hunting song, 'D've Ken John Peel?', written by his friend John Graves. John Peel was born in Cumberland in 1776 and died in 1854 after a fall. His parents were yeoman farmers who were keen on hunting but in the fells, hunting of the fox usually took place on foot. John Peel kept hounds and hunted with twelve couples from around 1799. Like so many of his contemporaries, he gained a reputation for heavy drinking. It is thought that at one stage he worked on Lord Lonsdale's Caldbeck Estate. One day, he eloped with a local girl, Mary White, to Gretna Green. Unfortunately, his grave in Caldbeck churchyard was vandalized by anti-fox-hunting campaigners during January 1977.

In the eighteenth century, the dress worn by the hunts varied considerably, as most packs of hounds were privately owned. Many men wore tricorn hats over their wigs. Later the fashion changed to wide-brimmed hats and then to top hats. Some hunt members were proud of their political allegiances and sported their relevant party colour on their hats; at that time it was blue for Whig and red for Tory. Although packs like the Berkeley in Gloucestershire had their own distinctive ornate, canary-coloured livery, and still do so, many others favoured green as the standard hunting colour for their long, loose-fitting coats. This may have followed from the earlier traditional use of the colour for stag hunting. For example, the hunt servants of the Duke of Beaufort always wore green and when the pack switched to fox-hunting in the late eighteenth century, they continued to wear the colour. However, the other members of the hunt distinguished themselves from the servants by wearing blue and buff coats, which were the colours of the Beaufort household livery at Badminton House, built in 1682.

The early riding breeches worn for hunting were made of buckskin but by the nineteenth century, both leather and then white cotton became more acceptable. It has been suggested that white breeches were first made fashionable by officers serving with the Duke of Wellington. They hunted in their uniforms and the contrasting scarlet jackets and white breeches were considered extremely elegant. A variety of riding boots were worn in the eighteenth century but generally they were long, loose-topped and over the knee. These hindered riding and it became the usual habit to turn down the top of the boot below the knee. This led to the appearance of a shorter boot with a coloured top, as now typified in a modern hunting boot.

As the nineteenth century progressed, correctness of dress became important and the scarlet jacket came into fashion. The use of scarlet as a colour for hunting coats had reputedly been first introduced much earlier by a tailor named Pink, after the American War of

Grey Hunter with
Groom and Hounds
(*Thomas Stringer*)

Independence ended in 1783. When the conflict ceased there was a
huge surplus of the scarlet cloth formerly used to make the uniforms
of the British soldiers. The legend has it that the entrepreneurial
spirit of Mr Pink led him to purchase the cloth, and one of the outlets
he pursued was to make hunting coats. He created a market for them
by promoting the concept that they were more readily visible in the
hunting field than the established green ones. The idea was
gradually accepted and the scarlet became known as hunting 'pink'.

By the 1850s, the scarlet jackets had become tight fitting and those
of the hunt servants (the huntsman and whippers-in) and honoured
prestigious members were adorned with five crested brass buttons
down the fronts. Although the jackets were similar, the hunt
servants despite their skill in the hunting field knew their place in
society and always behaved subserviently to the honoured members.
The Masters of the hunts were distinguished by wearing only four
buttons down the fronts of their jackets. A common factor with all the
coats was that they had two buttons on each cuff and two at the back
of the jacket.

Not all of the participants in a hunt were privileged to wear scarlet.
It was only the Master, honoured members and hunt servants who
wore it. The other followers wore black coats with silk top hats or
bowlers (called 'billycocks'). The honoured members, although
dressed in scarlet, wore top hats to distinguish them from the Master

and the hunt servants, who wore black velvet hunting caps. Only those who were concerned with the control of the hounds wore velvet caps. George III started the fashion of wearing the velvet cap in the hunting field. Previously, they were the standard headgear for mounted servants such as outriders. The scarlet jackets were worn with dark waistcoats beneath and a white stock (cravat) to match the white breeches; the hunting boots were black with a brown leather top.

Many of the private ancestral hunts, which survived into the nineteenth century, still adorned themselves with uniforms of their traditional colours, such as green, yellow or grey instead of scarlet. Some of the hunt servants wore six buttons on the tails of their coats to show they were part of the household of the owner of the hunt. Servants of the ancestral home, such as the footman, would also have worn six buttons as part of their traditional uniform.

The rising costs of fox-hunting and of maintaining a pack of foxhounds seriously reduced the number of private hunts by the

Father and Son with Huntsman at Browsholme Hall, Lancs. (*Benjamin Killingbeck*)

A Master with his
Hounds (*Charles
Hancock*)

early nineteenth century. The hunts started to be supported by
members to help the Master with costs. The members consisted
mainly of the squirearchy and the wealthier tenant farmers but later,
men who had acquired wealth from the Industrial Revolution joined
them. These hunts were called 'subscription packs', as those who
hunted regularly guaranteed they would support the Master with a
subscription of an agreed sum. However, the local lord still normally
remained the Master of the hunt. Only squires were required to
subscribe; farmers who joined were not expected to contribute. As the
nineteenth century progressed, so did the number of subscription
packs. In 1810, there were twenty-four such packs out of a hundred
and by 1845 the number had risen to eighty-six out of a hundred
packs but by 1854 there were over ninety out of a hundred.

When the aristocratic hunts dwindled, controversies arose on how
to divide the former huge countries they hunted and share them
amongst the smaller subscription hunts. In the middle of the
nineteenth century, many arguments took place on the subject at
Boodle's Club in St James's, London, where members met to discuss
hunt countries. Eventually, the Masters of Foxhounds Association
was formed and assembled at Tattersalls for the first time in 1881.
The 8th Duke of Beaufort instigated the meeting in order to form a
ruling body for hunting and to establish co-operation between the
different packs of foxhounds. From that time onwards, the Masters of

Foxhounds Association has set the strict rules and standards which all recognized registered hunts must comply with. After the Masters of Foxhounds Association was formed, the influence of the smaller farmers in the hunts increased as that of the squires and wealthy tenant farmers diminished. The co-operation of the smaller farmers was needed to hunt over their land and they were encouraged to plant coverts, as well as to block the entrances to the foxes' earths the night before the hunt.

Earlier, the extension of canals and the coming of the railways in the middle of the nineteenth century were at first thought to be detrimental to the future of fox-hunting, as they cut through hunt territories. However, the fears proved groundless but the established character of hunting was changed as the railways allowed a wider spectrum of people to participate. The trains opened the sport to businessmen and industrialists who mixed and rode with the traditional country members of the hunts. Hunting also became a

Meeting before the Chase (*J.F. Herring, Sen.*)

fashionable sport with army officers in the later nineteenth century, the breed of the horse used for hunting being of particular interest and possible use to the cavalry.

At the Crossroads
(*H. Alken, Jun.*)

A shadow was cast over fox-hunting during the nineteenth century when the shameful practice of 'bagman' foxes was introduced. At the time, there was a shortage of foxes in England and foxes were imported from France, Germany and Holland. They were named 'bagman' foxes and most were sold through Leadenhall Street market in London. They were then called 'Leadenhallers' and were priced at ten to fifteen shillings each. Many sportsmen thought the idea disgraceful, as many of the foxes were transported under cruel conditions and arrived in a weak, distressed state unfit for hunting. In addition, when released from a bag in the countryside, they were not familiar with the territory, and many people considered it unsporting. Despite this, several Masters of Foxhounds took them to satisfy the demand for regular hunting in their territories. For example, during the season 1822–23, Squire Osbaldeston paid thirty shillings a brace for foxes which he purchased from a dealer in Tottenham Court Road. These were releaased for his hunt in Suffolk.

Poachers and some gamekeepers occasionally took foxes from their own localities and sold them to another part of England where there was a stronger hunting community. Secretly, gamekeepers were pleased at the shortage of foxes; much to the annoyance of the fox-hunting community, the gamekeepers destroyed many foxes by snaring and shooting them to protect their pheasants. They detested foxes because they often killed more game than they needed to satisfy their immediate hunger. Although the introduction of 'bagman' foxes temporarily increased the population of foxes in the country, the reverse occurred when some foxes imported from Germany brought mange with them. The practice of using alien foxes was then discontinued. The native population of foxes slowly increased, especially in areas where field voles were plentiful, as they were a main source of food.

In a similar manner to the early hunting of carted deer, a Mr Templer, who lived in Devon during the nineteenth century, kept half-tamed foxes to hunt. On a hunting day, one of his foxes would be released and chased but not killed. Skilfully, the hounds were called off at the last moment and the pack gained the nickname, 'the let-'em-alones'. The fox was then gathered up and taken back to the kennels. One such fox was hunted thirty-six times without apparently suffering any ill-effects. It probably adopted the attitude

Through the Gate
(*George Sebright*)

Gone Away
(*J.F. Herring, Sen.*)

of 'don't see 'ems' as regards the hounds. The half-tamed foxes were kept in the kennels with collars attached to long chains, and were reputed to wag their bushy tails when being fed. Mr Templer's pack later became the South Devon Hunt.

The latter part of the nineteenth century saw a potential hazard to fox-hunting. This was the widespread use of wire-netting and barbed wire to replace the more expensive post-and-rail fences on farms. Wire was introduced into England around 1858–59, and barbed wire in 1882. The wire presented a danger to both horse and rider. Many farmers marked the positions of the wire on their farms to assist the hunts, whilst the keener ones even built hunt jumps so that the wire could be by-passed. At the close of the nineteenth century most of the horses ridden were half-bred, out of working-class mares by thoroughbred stallions, to ensure they possessed stamina and strength when carrying a heavy huntsman. The hunter breeds varied depending upon the type of territory they were hunted over. The spectacle of the fox-hunt with men careering over the countryside was described by Oscar Wilde as 'the unspeakable in pursuit of the uneatable'.

The dawn of the twentieth century brought increasing support for fox-hunting and during the first decade it reached its zenith of popularity. It was now well regulated by the Masters of Foxhounds Association and each hunt was registered, together with the boundaries of its hunting country. Eventually, every individual hunt had a committee who selected and appointed the Master of the pack; later it often became the practice to have Joint-Masters and the appointments were made on an annual basis.

The Master of the pack employed the professional hunt servants and grooms. In addition, he was responsible for the day-to-day running of the hunt, such as the kennel breeding programme, and for maintaining good relations with all the landowners and farmers in his hunt territory. Most Masters were normally selected from those with a farming or large landowner background. The Master and committee always sought permission before hunting over anyone's private land, as fox-hunting was only possible by obtaining such a right. A minority of farmers opposed hunting, in case it damaged their property, but the hunt always compensated farmers for any accidental damage caused during the course of the hunt.

The foxhounds of the twentieth century were the result of a careful breeding selection which started around 1800, and the well-bred packs of hounds were based on English and Welsh blood lines. The Masters of Foxhounds Association contributed to the success by the maintenance of low stud fees for breeders. Modern foxhounds are strongly built with deep chests and their short coats have various colour combinations of white, black and tan. They are a pack animal

Gone Away. The Chase Commences (*Thomas Bretland*)

and are taught pack discipline from an early age, so that they are obedient and under firm control when near farm livestock. They are not taught to hunt – they do so by instinct – but they must be taught to hunt the fox solely, and no other quarry. All hunts now kennel their hounds as a pack and they are always fed together sharing a huge trough. Before the twentieth century, some packs were trencher-fed, which meant they were often kept and fed on individual hunt members' farms. On the date of the hunt, each member brought along his hound and the pack was reunited for the day. This procedure reduced the costs of the hunt but the hounds tended to display more individual behaviour when out hunting. Also, many of the hounds were less fit than the kennelled ones because the exercise given by individual keepers was variable.

During hunting, normally around fifteen to twenty couples of hounds run together. The practice of counting hounds in couples in fox-hunting may have originated from the time when they were tied together in pairs by their neck collars before release. The hounds are controlled by voice and the penetrating notes of the hunting horn. The horn is straight, around eight inches long and made of copper. In the past, some of the better-quality horns were finished with a contrasting silver mouthpiece. In the eighteenth century, a large circular horn of the French type was in common use but this was gradually replaced by the smaller more convenient horn. 'Tally-ho!', the huntsman's cry to the hounds on sighting a fox, may possibly have originated from a corruption of the French word *taiaut*, meaning 'he is raised'. It may also be based on earlier French equivalent words such as *taho, theau le hau* or *thia hillauo*. All of these sound rather similar when shouted, but the derivation remains obscure; some may have roots in Norman French.

The outbreak of the First World War dramatically affected fox-hunting and many hounds had to be put down and breeding program-mes halted. The few hunts that remained were cared for by lady members. The sport revived after the war but never reached pre-war levels again. During the nineteenth century there was a prejudice against ladies in the hunting field, as it was considered to be too rough and unladylike and therefore socially unacceptable. Also, many ladies were reluctant to hunt for fear of scratching their faces and ruining their complexions when crashing through high hedges. This risk was reduced whem more hedges started to be 'laid' in the nineteenth century. None of these things deterred the Marchioness of Salisbury who founded the Hatfield Hunt in Hertfordshire in 1800 and hunted with them for over forty years. She appears to have paid little attention to the social opinion of the day. As well as riding with hounds, she gambled heavily and when annoyed, her language was not noted for its gentility. She continued hunting well into her

seventies and even when nearly blind, she insisted on being strapped
to her saddle, and pluckily jumped over fences with the assistance of
a groom with a leading rein, who prompted her when to jump.

Another famous and notorious lady rider was Catherine Walters
(nicknamed 'Skittles') who was accepted into the elite Quorn Hunt in
the late nineteenth century, despite her former lowly background
and squalid upbringing in the dockland area of Liverpool. She was
born in 1839 and her nickname arose from her early days when she
worked in public houses setting up skittles in the alleys. However, by
her charm and a succession of aristocratic lovers she rose quickly
through society and became not only one of the most renowned
demi-mondaines but also one of the most brilliant riders of her day.
Although partially illiterate, she entertained such famous public
figures as the Prince of Wales and Gladstone. She died in 1920. In
earlier times, both Queen Elizabeth I and Queen Anne were keen
huntswomen, but then there was no social stigma attached to ladies
riding; it only appeared a century later.

The few ladies who hunted in Victorian times rode side-saddle with
the hem of their awkward ankle-length, wide double skirts weighted
down with lead weights. The horse had to be held completely still for
the lady to mount. Hats were soft and trimmed with feathers, and the
whole dress was impractical and dangerous for riding. Despite this,
women could not wear breeches as it was against all social
conventions. The early side-saddles offered little security to the rider,
especially when changing direction quickly or jumping. These
saddles were fitted with two pommels high up on the near side of the
saddle, one for use on either side of the right leg. In a fall, the
side-saddle was dangerous unless the rider was thrown clear, as the
protruding pommels were liable to cause serious injury if the horse
rolled over. A third pommel was added during the second half of the
nineteenth century below the original two. It had the shape of a
downward curving horn. This, known as a 'leaping head', positioned
just above the left leg, allowed the rider to make contact with it when
needed with the upper part of the left thigh to obtain the necessary
grip. This gave a vastly improved confident 'seat' when jumping.
Later the very top pommel of the three was found to be superfluous
and was discarded. The saddle therefore reverted to two pommels, as
in the earlier design, but both were now positioned much lower on the
side of the saddle. Despite the improvements, it remained difficult to
ride a refusing horse side-saddle, and a very bold mount was
desirable.

By the end of the nineteenth century, the safety split half-skirt or
apron came into fashion which covered the left stirrup and foot by
about three inches. It was designed by Mrs Alice Hayes. The skirt
buttoned down on the offside when the lady stood on the ground, but

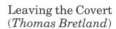
Leaving the Covert
(*Thomas Bretland*)

the split was unbuttoned when the lady was mounted. The skirt was shaped so that it could not catch on the pommel of the side-saddle in the event of a fall and the rider could not be dragged. It was considered more decent than the earlier version, known as the fig-leaf, which was designed to rip off in an emergency and remain attached to the pommel of the saddle, whilst the lady fell away from the horse in her petticoat. An amusing cartoon in *Punch* in 1860 depicted such an incident and carried the caption, 'Miss Diana strips off at a fence and leaves the better half of her habit on the pommels of her saddle'.

In the eighteenth century, ladies' mounts were taught never to trot, as this was a most uncomfortable action for the rider. The horses were schooled only to walk or canter. Towards the end of the nineteenth century, the number of ladies who hunted increased considerably and it became quite fashionable to hunt. Horses were then allowed to trot because this was a more comfortable gait for the horse when travelling over a distance. Ladies were not expected to subscribe to the packs until the 1890s, and then for many years the fee remained at a lower rate than that of the gentlemen. As regards dress, at the beginning of the twentieth century social etiquette demanded that a married lady wore a top hat when hunting, whilst an unmarried lady wore a round bowler, often with a short veil. Following modern safety regulations, most who now hunt protect their heads with a fibreglass skull-cap secured firmly with a harness and strap.

A great exponent of riding with the side-saddle in the twentieth century was the Lady Helena Fitzwilliam, who hunted with the Pytchley. She was tragically killed in the hunting field. Many farmers' daughters started to take up hunting as the twentieth century progressed. During the Second World War many of the hunts were looked after, as in the First World War, by lady members, and several became Masters. After the end of the war, in 1945, riding astride came into fashion. Previously, it had been greatly resisted as it was deemed to be unfeminine and unattractive. Many businesswomen also joined the hunts and by 1992 the number of Lady Masters (or Joint-Masters) had risen to nearly twenty-five per cent of the total of registered hunts.

Although many of the hunts were not active during the Second World War, the names of many foxhound packs were kept alive at sea by the Royal Navy's Hunt Class destroyers, as each vessel was named after a pack of foxhounds. Fox-hunting revived again after the war, but a strong campaign was mounted to prohibit it. A Private Member's Bill was debated in Parliament in 1949 but the bill was defeated by 214 votes to 101. There have been many such campaigns since and the latest bill presented to the House of Commons in 1992 was defeated by just twelve votes. It is obvious that when the next vote is held, the result in the House of Commons may be in favour of

The Chase (*J.N. Sartorius*)

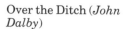
Over the Ditch (*John Dalby*)

abolition or restriction. Several county councils are already banning hunting on public land.

In the twentieth century, fox-hunting gained strong royal patronage, as Edward VII, Edward VIII, George VI, Queen Elizabeth II (when Princess Elizabeth) and Prince Charles all participated. This may have led many people living in city and suburban areas to view fox-hunting as an elitest sport, although it now embraces all classes of society. Royals, lords, landowners, farmers, jockeys, businessmen and women and local country people and many others go hunting. A few hunts allow a visitor to hire a hunter for the day and pay a 'cap' fee for a day's hunting, irrespective of his or her position in society. In addition, the hunt attracts many keen car and foot followers who do not wish to be mounted.

During a hunt, the majority of the foxes that are pursued escape unharmed, and many who go hunting never witness a kill. However, foxes are killed, which is why so many farmers allow the hunt over their land. The cunning intelligence of the wild fox and its familiarity with the local countryside, instinctively lead it to double-back on its tracks, walk along walls, run in water or mingle with the farm livestock to confuse its scent to the following hounds. On occasions, the fox seeks refuge in trees and even in dwellings. If caught the fox has no chance to escape wounded; it is always killed outright and very quickly by the single leading hound which reaches it first. The hound snaps the spinal cord with a powerful bite, as a terrier kills a rat. Hounds are four or five times heavier than the quarry. A fox is never 'torn' to pieces alive, as so many people believe nowadays.

Traditionally, the head of the fox (the 'mask'), the tail (the 'brush') and feet (the 'pads') were given by the Master to members of the hunt as trophies. Another gruesome practice, known as 'blooding', involved smearing the blood of the dead fox on any novice present, which may have been a child. The blood was never washed from the face but was allowed to wear off. The procedure was first introduced for stag hunting by James I. However, this ritual no longer takes place.

In the early aristocratic hunts and the more elaborate wealthy Victorian hunts, it was the custom to offer the hunting guests the hunt breakfast, when they assembled in the morning for the meet. This was often held in the Great Hall of the large imposing residence or manor house of the host. It was followed by the ritual of a drink from the stirrup cup to fortify participants for the day's hunting. The stirrup cup, made of silver in the shape of a fox or hound's head, would be passed from the host to the Master of the hunt, then to the huntsman, next to the whippers-in and down the line in order of importance to the various guests. The hunt would then depart at the command of the Master from the host's house to commence the day's sport. Later, it became more usual for the hunt to meet outside a

Crossing a Stream
(*John Dalby*)

Fall at the Fence
(*John Dalby*)

country pub, or on the village green, and for large hunts the drinks were passed around in glasses from a tray. The hunting would take place at various locations within the hunt's recognized country, to control the foxes evenly in the region.

As well as commanding the hunt, the Master also plans the strategy for the day's sport. Prior to departure, the permission of all the landowners and farmers to ride over their land would, of course, have been obtained and the best route for jumping obstacles ascertained to minimize damage to fences and other property. Unlike the early days of fox-hunting, the riders generally no longer take their own 'line' across country. Protocol demands all gates are firmly shut as the hunt passes through farmland, to keep stock secure. The Master relies on the co-operation of the local farmers and landowners to stop temporarily any natural earths on their land, where a fox might take refuge. This is usually done with clods of soil and sticks. In the eighteenth and nineteenth centuries, earth-stoppers were paid to perform this task. It is now illegal to block any badger sett entrances unless only temporary loose material is used.

During the hunt, the professional huntsman assists the Master and he is responsible for controlling the hounds as well as hunting the quarry. In this task, the huntsman is assisted by the whippers-in, who bring back straying hounds to the pack and help to reconnoitre

The Quorn Hunt
taking the Whissen-
dine *(John Dalby)*

the land. The rest of the field, either on horseback or on foot, are
called the followers of the hunt and only play the role of spectators.
The riders enjoy the exhilarating gallop during the chase, while those
on foot enjoy watching the hounds at work. Hounds hunt by scent
following the 'drag' of the fox. However, the fox has first to be located
and so the hunt 'draws' (searches) the coverts where the quarry is
likely to be found.

The excited cry of the hounds heralds the discovery of a fox, and the
sound of the huntsman's horn in a rapid series of notes, together with
shouts of 'Tally-ho!' denotes that the quarry has left cover. The chase
commences with the huntsman casting the hounds on the line of the
departing fox. However, in many cases the intrigue of the fox enables
it to escape unharmed, or to find refuge in an 'unstopped' natural
earth although not all quarries are lost and a fox may be caught and
killed in the open.

When a fox runs to ground it may be left in peace, or at the request
of the farmer or landowner, a terrier may be used to locate it and the
fox is dug out. As soon as the fox is exposed in the ground, it must be
immediately destroyed with a humane killer by the terrier man, who
is a hunt servant bound by the strict rules of the Masters of
Foxhounds Association. In the past, it was customary to 'bolt' the fox
from the earth and after giving it a fair and sporting chance of
escape, the chase recommenced. This procedure is now banned by the
Masters of Foxhounds Association's *Code of Good Hunting Practice*,

issued in 1992, and a fox may no longer be hunted again after going to earth. Traditionally, hunts are allowed to pursue a fox when it enters a neighbouring hunt's territory but if it goes to ground the hunt is abandoned. The fox-hunting season starts traditionally on 1st November and continues until the following March. The two hundred registered packs of foxhounds in Britain kill around eighteen thousand foxes a year, although obviously the tally varies from year to year.

After harvest time in August and before the proper season starts, cub-hunting takes place. These are the young foxes reared during the summer but by the time they are hunted in the autumn, they have grown to roughly the same size as the mature foxes. Cub-hunting is usually carried out at the request of farmers and landowners who wish to cull a percentage of the young foxes and disperse the others more evenly over the countryside. Some sheep farmers request the cub-hunting to take place in April. Most cub-hunting takes place early in the morning, when the scent of the fox is at its strongest. The night before, the hunt organizers arrange to stop any natural earths in the area of the covert to be hunted. Most kills are made in covert to prevent disturbance to farm stock still out in the fields. This is done by the Master selecting and posting both mounted and foot followers around the covert, to wait for any cub which might break cover after the hounds are sent in. The main task of the people surrounding the covert is the 'holding-up' of the fox (a term used for 'turning-back'). The fox is discouraged from leaving the covert by people making a noise with

Full Cry with Lady Rider (Ben Herring, Jun.)

Full Cry over the
Fence (*S.J.E. Jones*)

their voices, or the tapping sound of sticks or whips, or the cracking of whips. The hunting code prohibits all other means.

If a fox escapes, then hounds may be allowed to pursue it, depending upon the particular circumstances in the surrounding fields, such as the presence of grazing stock. The more resolute and fit young foxes are normally the ones that escape – a case of survival of the fittest. The weaker animals tend to remain in the covert, and are killed by the hounds who often surround them (known as 'mobbing') without giving them any chance of escape. Any cub which finds an unstopped hole will either be flushed out with a terrier, or dug out and killed. Cub-hunting is the most unsporting and distressing part of fox-hunting but the huntsmen say it forms an important part of general fox control. The League Against Cruel Sports states that it is done 'to teach young inexperienced foxhounds the tricks of a grisly trade before the start of the fox-hunting season proper in November'. The League estimates that around six thousand fox cubs are killed each year in this way. Without doubt the hunts take advantage of the cub-hunting season to blood their young hounds, ie make their first kill, and educate them alongside the older experienced foxhounds. Usually, a total of around twenty or thirty couples of hounds is involved in the cub-hunt.

As well as hunting, many social activities are arranged by the

Near the End (*James Pollard*)

hunts which are enjoyed by the local community and at the same time raise funds. The social highlight of the hunt, the Hunt Ball, when introduced in the eighteenth century did little to create a unified rural society. It was often held, throughout the eighteenth and nineteenth centuries, at a stately home and only the nobility and gentry were invited. At the end of the eighteenth century, these formed around ninety per cent of the hunt members, and farmers just ten per cent. The farmers were rarely invited to wear scarlet when hunting and never attended the Hunt Ball. Later, hunt dinners were held to include a wider social mix of people, although these were restricted to men only. In addition, many hunts held dinners solely for the farmers.

As the twentieth century progressed, many Hunt Supporters Clubs were formed and nowadays most of their members are those who follow the hunt on foot or in cars. They organize social events to bring the rural community together during club suppers, dances, cheese and wine parties, puppy shows, skittle matches, whist drives, horse trials and similar fund-raising activities. It is now also a common sight to see a huntsman and hounds at many annual agricultural shows. Often children are invited to mingle with the hounds to show how well-disciplined and gentle they are in public.

Hunt point-to-point races with their amateur lady and gentleman

Hounds at the Kill
(*J.N. Sartorius*)

riders have for many years provided one of the main financial benefits for the hunt. They take place at the end of the hunting season, from early February to the end of May. Only horses that have hunted at least eight times, with a pack of hounds, in the current season are qualified to enter. They must possess certificates signed by the Master of their hunt to verify this. It is reputed that the first point-to-point race took place at Nacton in Suffolk, in 1803. In the eighteenth century, races were run across long distances of country on the flat, without a set course, and the event was always won by hard-riding and the horse with the best stamina.

When the speed of the thoroughbred was introduced, it was decided it would be better to run the race along a set course and that racing over obstacles, such as hedges and fences, would add to the excitement. In order that the riders knew the correct course, prominent features of the countryside, such as church towers or steeples, were used and the horses ran in a direct line from the starting point to the distant point in view, the tower or steeple. At first these races were run as a match between two riders but later more riders took part. The early races were rough, with no quarter being given to the other rider. They were also extremely cruel to the horses, which were often hard-ridden to exhaustion. Many who valued their horses refused to participate in such events. Regulations for the running of point-to-point races were drawn up in 1866 and detailed rules introduced. This initiated an upsurge in point-to-point racing during the 1870s, and by the turn of the century nearly all hunts ran their own meetings. In the early 1990s the average crowd at individual point-to-point meetings was three thousand to four thousand.

The sport of fox-hunting led not only to amateur point-to-point racing but also to modern professional steeplechasing or National Hunt racing, which was a marriage of hunting (jumping) and flat racing. National Hunt racing was both over hurdles and larger fences with open ditches and water jumps. Fox-hunting was also linked to the rise of show jumping, as evidenced by the scarlet jackets worn by the riders of today, and cross-country and hunter trials evolved from fox-hunting too. The founding of the Pony Clubs for young riders in 1929 developed the potential hunt members of the future, who often attended cub-hunts. Children were taught not only how to ride and jump but stable work and how to care for horses as well. Pony Clubs and similar Pony Societies were formed all over England in subsequent years, and these have been the main instigators of

Lady's Riding Habit in Mid-19th Century (*James Loder*)

Steeplechasing in 19th Century (*J.F. Herring, Jun.*)

keeping various pony breeds pure. Most Pony Clubs hold an annual camp for their members, in August or sometimes early September.

Drag hunting, which is similar to fox-hunting but without a final kill, was probably first experimented with as early as the seventeenth century. In this sport, a prepared trail of a strong-smelling scent is laid for the hounds to follow instead of a live quarry. The riders participate purely for the pleasure and excitement of riding across country.

Initially, such trails were based on aniseed mixed with urine. This yielded a strong attractive smell for the hounds, with the advantage that the scent persisted as it had a slow rate of evaporation. It was normally laid on the ground by dragging along a soaked padded sock or sack. This was done either by towing it along on foot or behind a horseman, about twenty minutes before the departure of the field. Later, alternative chemical scents were developed which were more durable and could be put down between two and three hours before the drag meeting took place. Breaks were made in the trail at intervals, so that the hounds had to work to pick up the line again.

Modern drag hunting started in earnest when Oxford and Cambridge Universities formed separate packs during the second half of the nineteenth century. They were quickly followed by the military, as the Household Brigade became interested in the sport in 1863. By 1870, both the Royal Artillery in Woolwich and the Royal Military Academy at Sandhurst had formed drag packs. Other packs were founded in the twentieth century, and the Mid-Surrey Farmers' Drag Hounds acquired an excellent reputation during the 1950s. All the packs were registered with the Masters of Drag Hounds Association.

Drag hunting became an ideal sport during the twentieth century, as more roads, including motorways, were built and towns sprawled into the countryside. The city and town folk found they could readily travel to a drag hunt meeting and the hunt, unlike fox-hunting, took only about three hours. They were always guaranteed a run. It was an ideal opportunity for business and town people to get into the fresh air and ride across country. The riders although only following the hounds along an artificial trail, still had to be disciplined and warned not to ride over the hounds. This would have interfered with their concentration and ability to track quietly the laid lure trail. The drag hunt season started in the Spring, during the middle of March. Drag hunting may become even more popular as a substitute for fox-hunting with hounds, should the latter ever be banned. However, this depends on whether farmers would still give permission for their land to be used, as the previous incentive of reducing the number of foxes would no longer apply.

As the twentieth century has progressed, many foxes have adapted to living in a completely urban environment; previously they kept exclusively to the town commons. They are found in cities and towns throughout England. Some councils employ marksmen to shoot them on wasteland when their number is considered excessive. It is thought that refuse bins containing discarded food attract foxes to urban areas. They also obtain food from garden bird tables and some people leave out scraps for them. Mice, voles and hedgehogs form another part of their diet when the foxes hunt them in churchyards and wasteland. After a rainstorm, foxes enjoy eating earthworms, slugs and beetles. They are excellent scavengers and encounter little difficulty in finding sustenance within the urban environment. Although not strictly nocturnal, foxes rest during the day under any convenient cover, such as beneath garden sheds, on wasteland, in churchyards, grounds of nursing homes and other peaceful gardens.

A few years ago, research work at Bristol estimated there were about five hundred adult foxes in the city and they produced around a thousand cubs a year. Town foxes breed in any convenient location, such as in cemeteries, on rubbish tips and land along railway cuttings. Approximately sixty per cent of the cubs die, the most common cause of death being the motor car. By nature, foxes only scent the air for signs of danger and they tend to freeze momentarily when caught in headlights. However, enough foxes survive to ensure that the urban fox is here to stay whatever happens in the future to his countryside cousin. The traditional countryside of the fox is under constant threat and England has lost more than a million acres of farmland since 1945. Much has disappeared under concrete and asphalt to satisfy the insatiable demand for housing, roads and industrial development. In addition, more than a quarter of the country's rough grazing land has been destroyed by urban development. All these factors suggest that in future more foxes will live in urban sprawls. Even in built-up areas where the fox abounds, few people manage to catch a glimpse of this elusive, cunning creature. No wonder his countryside cousin so frequently outwits the hounds.

Otter-hunting (*Charles Cooper Henderson*)

8   Otter and Mink-hunting

For many centuries, otters were considered to be noxious vermin. It is now a different story and most people view the river otter as a delightful, playful creature, as exemplified in the tales of *Tarka the Otter* and *Ring of Bright Water*. Otters appear to enjoy playing games in the company of their cubs, or sometimes with other otters, and even amuse themselves when alone. In the latter case, they often hold a pebble between their forepaws when in the water, toss it into the air and retrieve it by diving under the surface. They also delight in sliding down muddy river banks and snow drifts as a form of easy locomotion, and engage in many other fascinating activities. When in the water, otters are fast, acrobatic swimmers owing to their broad webbed feet and powerful tail; they glide silently beneath the surface barely causing a ripple. This ability makes them extremely effective and tenacious hunters of fish which they chase mainly by sight. They also feed on frogs, water fowl (by pulling them below the surface) and eels. Most of their hunting takes place at night and they can travel overland as well as in water. When on the ground they are able to stand upright by balancing themselves on their hind feet and outstretched tails. This pose, known as tripoding, allows the otter to scan the landscape.

Otters are members of the weasel family, although the male is commonly known as the water-dog. The fully grown male (the dog) weighs around 23 lb and the female (the bitch) 16 lb. The length varies between 3½ and 4 feet. Both the bodies and tapering tails are long to give a streamlined appearance but the legs are short, as expected for a relative of the weasel and stoat.

Otters move many miles up or down river when food becomes short in their immediate vicinity, so they are not permanent residents of a single retreat. They are secretive creatures, and during the daytime they nestle along river-banks in hollows or under tree roots; these lying-up places are called 'holts' or 'hovers'. Otters may have several of these temporary refuges along a stretch of river-bank. As a result, the unpredictable movements of the otters made them difficult to find when they were hunted as a pest in the past. They had no natural predators to control their numbers and man assumed this role.

However, the hunting of the otter was banned in 1978 throughout England and Wales; later the Wildlife and Countryside Act (1981) protected them throughout the whole of the United Kingdom. The reason for the protection was the decline in their numbers during the second half of the twentieth century, despite having a fairly stable population during the first half of the century. According to a report of the British Mammal Society, in *Oryx* in 1969, the hunting of the otter this century would not have been the cause of the significant population decrease. It is now rare to see an otter in the wild. The few who survive are most likely to be found in the west of England. They were once a common sight on the Norfolk Broads. The harsh winter of 1962–63 severely affected the numbers in the south and east. New drainage schemes, initiated by various authorities, also influenced otter populations at that time, as less fish was available for food. In addition, otters retreated from many lowland rivers due to increasing human disturbance. The industrial pollution of rivers also played a significant role in their continuing demise. Traces of pesticides, detergents and chemical products containing heavy metals such as lead, cadmium and mercury contaminated rivers. The chemicals used in sheep dips were especially lethal to the otter.

The various chemical pollutants affected the fish which passed to the otter via the food chain. It is likely that some of these contaminants reduced the breeding potential of the otter. In addition, the detergents may have damaged the effectiveness of the waterproof coats of the otters and it would have been more difficult for them to survive the damp and cold. In Norfolk, the widespread use of eel nets by fishermen devastated the otter population. The otters were attracted to the wide funnel entrances of the nets, probably in search of the eels inside. Unfortunately, once inside the otters were unable to find a way out and they quickly drowned. The large lungs of the otter take in only enough air, before it dives, to allow it to stay submerged for three or four minutes.

Otters breed in special underground holts, situated well above the water level of the winter floods to save the vulnerable cubs from drowning. These breeding holts are often under the roots of trees – ash trees are favourites – and the entrances are well-concealed with the natural riverside vegetation. Otters appear to have no well-defined breeding season. They normally produce up to three cubs in a year; the lifespan in the wild is difficult to assess but the average is probably well under ten years.

Many steps have now been taken to safeguard the environment for the otter, and several otter havens have been established in various parts of England. They were founded with the co-operation of the water authorities and landowners. The Otter Trust based at

Earsham on the River Waveney along the Suffolk/Norfolk border now breeds some otters for release to the wild. A stretch of the river was dredged to construct a series of large pens for them. Some of these pens were situated in a remote area, well away from people, so that the otters were left in peace for several months to acclimatize before release to the wild, perhaps to re-colonize their old haunts. The Vincent Wildlife Trust has also established havens, mainly in the west and north of England.

Before otters were protected, they had been hunted by man for at least seven to eight hundred years. The devastation of game-fish in rivers, such as salmon and trout, was the main reason for the otters' persecution. Many were trapped by water bailiffs because they caused considerable damage to fish hatcheries at spawning time. Otters were sometimes captured for their skins to make linings for coats in the fifteenth and sixteenth centuries. The trapping was not widespread in England but in the Shetland Isles it was more prevalent. The trade stopped in the seventeenth century, when the greater abundance of otters in northern Europe made it more economic to import pelts. Later, during the nineteenth century, otter pelts were imported from North America.

In 1566 the otter was officially classified as vermin by an Act of Parliament and parish officials offered bounties of between sixpence and one shilling for dead otters. The precise amount varied in different parts of England, and was set by the local authorities. As well as for the protection of fish in rivers, the passing of the Act was probably encouraged by the wealthier members of society to preserve the fish stocks kept in their game-ponds on their estates. This was especially important to owners of such ponds who lived far away from a river or the sea. At the time the fish were a very important commodity for the household. Otters were caught mainly by trapping, entangling with nets, hunting with otter-hounds and spearing. Much later, during the eighteenth century, the gun was used and this considerably reduced for a time the otter population in England.

The hunting with dogs had begun many centuries earlier. It is reported that King Henry II in 1175 made Roger Follo responsible for a small pack of otter-hounds. Other royalty were to continue the tradition but only showed a passing interest in otter-hunting as a sport. King John, in 1212, was known to have a pack of six couples of otter-hounds and they were hunted in Somerset. Later kings, such as Edward II in 1367 and Richard II in 1377, kept the same number of hounds. There were still only six couples in the royal pack when Richard III took the throne in 1483.

Otter-hunting received a boost in Tudor times after Henry VIII became king in 1509, as he showed more enthusiasm for the sport.

He appointed himself Master of Otter-hounds. In addition, his daughter, when she later became Queen Elizabeth I, gained the distinction of being the first Lady of Otter-hounds. Afterwards the sport grew slowly and became more established and popular, although it never rivalled the alternative hunting sports. It remained reasonably popular until the end of the seventeenth century but then suffered periods of decline. It reached its peak following as a rural sporting pastime during the last decade of the nineteenth century, when there were about twenty packs of otter-hounds. Devon claimed one of the oldest packs, established in 1825, the Dartmoor Otter-hounds. This was quickly followed by the Culmstock, formed in 1837 by Mr W.P. Collier. The Reverend Hylton Wyburgh became Master of a pack in Cumberland during 1830 which became known as the West Cumberland.

James I, as an experiment, instead of hunting the otter used tame otters to hunt the salmon for him on his royal estates, at the beginning of the seventeenth century. The technique had previously been exploited in Scotland and in other parts of the world. Otters were tamed and taught to perform the task from an early age. The training was probably not too difficult as otters are, by nature, persistent hunters of fish. After capturing a salmon they often bring their prey to the bank and leave it, probably after being disturbed, with just a small bite taken out of it. It would therefore have been easy to collect the discarded fish along the river-banks on the royal estates where there would have been an abundance of salmon.

James I hunted otters as well and to encourage the sport he ordered this to be done only with hounds; trapping was banned. He even commanded men working in the corn-grinding mills to cease work on his hunting days, so that the river levels were not affected by using water power. In areas such as Norfolk where otters were plentiful at the time, he ordered the local authorities to raise money to support the pack of otter-hounds.

The otter-hounds used during the past centuries were of uncertain ancestry but most were large dogs up to twenty-seven inches at the shoulder. It was thought that the original hounds were bred from the Southern hound, the Saint Hubert and the French griffon. The breed of the bloodhound was introduced to enhance the scenting ability, and that of the water spaniel, amongst several other strains, to improve performance in the water. The otter-hound needed to be a powerful swimmer and because it spent a long time in rivers, its dense water-resistant undercoat with an outer long shaggy one was essential. The hound also had large webbed feet and abundant stamina. Much otter-hunting took place in Wales and inevitably the blood of the rough-coated Welsh foxhound was introduced.

When the otter was hunted, only small packs of around eight

couples were used. The otter left a persistent exceedingly pungent scent which enabled the hounds to follow it over boggy terrain and even over the surface of water. Until about 1830 and in some areas much later, long spears were used to kill an otter when the hounds tracked it down in the water. It was unusual for the hounds to attempt to kill an otter whilst swimming. The huntsman waited until the otter came to the surface for air and then struck. The spears were occasionally thrown javelin-wise. The hunter had to stand in the water in the path of the otter and estimate where it was likely to rise to the surface. Otters were also speared on land when hidden under cover of river rushes and long grass, but this often led to a hound being accidentally spiked in the general excitement. When an otter was successfully impaled it was lifted high in the air on the end of the spear in triumph. The spears used were about twelve feet long and the single-prong metal head had two sharp barbs. In the seventeenth century, two-prong spears were sometimes used because it was thought they gave a better chance of hitting the elusive quarry. However, the extra weight of the head impeded the easy handling of the weapon. After 1830, the feeling grew that the use of a spear was unsportsmanlike. It was then only resorted to when the hounds had surrounded the otter. This was to save the hounds from needless injury from the fierce bite of the cornered otter. The spear was eventually totally discarded in the 1860s. The netting of otters was also banned as previously nets were sometimes hurriedly stretched across a river to prevent the otter reaching deep water.

During the late eighteenth century, otter-hunting attracted a wide cross-section of the rural community. As no horse was needed, poorer agricultural workers took up the sport and mixed with lords, squires and farmers. Very occasionally, after a successful kill, the heart of the otter was taken, dressed and eaten by some of the hunt. A report from 1796 suggested that it was delicious. Many of the gentry frowned upon hunting in the company of the common workers and in the early part of the nineteenth century the sport became less fashionable. However, 'Jack Russell', the notorious and famous fox-hunting parson from Devon, was not so particular and continued to pursue the otter when not hunting the fox. A contributory factor to the decline in otter-hunting was that the numbers of otters had decreased markedly owing to the excessive hunting at this time. Fortunately, they were not persecuted nearly to extinction as had earlier been the fate of the pine marten and polecat. Otter-hunting therefore fell in popularity for many decades until a late Victorian revival. In 1892 there were fifteen packs of otter-hounds and this figure rose to twenty-three by 1908. This surge in popularity lasted until the outbreak of the First World War in 1914.

All packs of otter-hounds this century came under the jurisdiction of the Masters of Otter-hounds Association. It became a true established field sport and the hunting season was set from mid-April to about the middle of September. This was to avoid hunting in the middle of winter. The otter has no fixed breeding season but it saved the otter-hounds from having to plunge into icy waters. In former years, there was no official hunting season and the quarry was hunted without a sporting instinct and was given no chance to bolt if found in a refuge in a river-bank. At the beginning of a modern hunt in this century, the first task was for the hounds to find the 'drag' (scent trail) of the otter. This was done by the hounds searching along the long stretches of river-banks. Although the scent was strong, it was no easy task to discover. It was usually several hours old, unless the hunt started very early in the morning. The otter would have returned to one of its holts before dawn, after meandering for several miles during the night. The scent trail was long, and even when picked up by the hounds, it could easily be followed in the opposite direction away from the otter. When the scent was lost, it was not easy to find again and many otter-hunts, around fifty per cent, ended in failure.

The hunting of the otter was an arduous pursuit and demanded considerable stamina from the huntsman and followers who often walked perhaps ten to fifteen miles over difficult, wet terrain. Many carried long poles to help them negotiate rivers and boggy ditches. A welcome respite occurred when the hounds swam in the river because the water slowed their progress. This enabled the followers to regain their breath whilst watching the hounds at work. After an otter was found, it was chased over land and in water. The excitement of the pursuit no doubt gave renewed energy to the weary followers. The huntsman kept in touch with his pack of hounds with his hunting horn, in similar fashion to the stag and fox-hunter.

When the otter heard the hounds were getting close, it would often hide in a hole in the river-bank or other temporary refuge. If discovered, the huntsman would attempt to make the otter 'bolt', either by the use of a terrier or by digging out. After the otter had been put to flight, it was given time and a fair chance to escape before the hounds were laid on the trail again. In the course of bolting the otter, the terrier unavoidably became contaminated with the pungent scent of the otter and it was not unknown for the hounds to attack the terrier by mistake. If the otter was finally cornered on land, it was killed by the hounds.

The otter-hunters dressed in a traditional hunt uniform which was both neat and practical. The bowler hat became part of this, although caps of various colours were also worn. The jackets were always blue, and underneath waistcoats of varying colours were donned. The uniform was completed with breeches, thick stockings and boots. The boots often had holes made in them to let water escape after wading across streams. The obvious disadvantage of these was that they also allowed water in, even when the water level was below the top of the boot.

During the First World War, the otter population increased as they were left relatively undisturbed. After the war, many were killed by gamekeepers again to control their numbers in order to protect fish stocks. Hunting also resumed. The outbreak of the Second World War in 1939 brought about a similar cycle of events; the otter population expanded as few were culled. When that war ended, hunting again resumed but gradually the otter-hound was used much less. The Masters of Otter-hounds could no longer afford the expense of breeding and rearing their own packs for hunting. Many started to hunt with large foxhounds and cross-breeds with terriers instead.

In the 1950s, otter-hunting still took place in many parts of England, Wales and south-west Scotland. The total number of packs in existence was thirteen. They hunted on average about forty-five days a year and between them killed around two hundred otters. It was just after this period that otter populations fell dramatically, mainly as a result of pollution of rivers. The Midlands of England was particularly badly affected. Otter-hunting therefore declined and at the beginning of the 1960s only fifty were killed by all the hunts combined.

In 1964, the general policy was to hunt otters purely for sport but not to kill them. This was done fourteen years before otter-hunting was officially banned by Parliament. The 1964 policy enabled many of the packs of hounds to be kept together and exercised, whilst at the same time conserving the otter, although probably terrifying it. However, this was not to last long and the growing scarcity of otters took its toll on this new variation of the sport. In the late 1960s and early 1970s, many hunts such as the Crowhurst in Surrey, the Malton in Yorkshire, the Eastern Counties and the Buckinghamshire, ceased to function. The Hawkesmoor in Shropshire, the Pembroke and Carmarthen in Wales and one of the oldest established, the Kendal and District in the Lake District, followed shortly after and ended hunting. The Master of the Kendal and District, just before its closure, decided to form the Otter-hound Club of Great Britain to conserve the otter-hound breed which by this time had become rare and has remained so today. The breed has been maintained purely for showing.

By 1972, nine hunts still remained. The hunts in the West Country were the longest to survive, such as the Dartmoor, the Culmstock and the Courtney Tracy. However, all hunts in England disbanded before the otter was made a protected species. This was done to help conserve the otter whose population has been so devastated. Surprisingly, otter-hunting lasted longer in Scotland, even though it was not a traditional Highland sport. An otter-hound pack was imported into the Isle of Mull to hunt there in 1975. The move was strongly opposed by the Scottish Wildlife Trust; otter-hunting had previously only taken place widely in south-west Scotland. In England, not all the otter-hunts were dispersed, as some re-organized themselves to hunt the mink, another relative of the weasel.

Mink were originally imported into England from the United States of America in 1929 to breed on fur farms, and the practice continued in the following years. The fur of the mink was highly valued and that of the American mink was considered to be very luxurious. Unfortunately, several escaped, and many were released into the wild in the 1950s by animal liberation groups, to wreak a trail of destruction on other wildlife. The early mink escapees had little difficulty in adapting to the wild and quickly established a self-sustaining feral population along the River Teign in Devon. By the 1960s, other groups of releases and escapees from mink farms had become colonized in waterside and woodland habitats in many parts of the United Kingdom. In England, parts of East Anglia and the north Midlands were affected as well as the south of England. Parts of Dyfed in Wales and some areas of southern and north-east Scotland, together with the Western Isles, were also invaded by the mink. The mink thrived in the United Kingdom because there are no natural predators to control their numbers. In America, however, large birds of prey and carnivores restrict the mink population in the wild.

Mink kill wildlife, even when they are not hungry, and so are classified as ruthless and ferocious pests. They devastate populations of fish and game-birds and also eat small mammals, frogs, moorhens, coots, ducklings and occasionally free-range poultry. They are semi-aquatic and more nocturnal than the otter but are only a fraction of their size. Mink are only about eighteen inches to two feet long with short tails of five to nine inches. Otters are nearly ten times heavier. Mink sometimes swim across rivers to islands that are wildlife sanctuaries and cause chaos. It was once thought that mink drove otters away from their traditional territories but this is no longer thought to be true. The superior size of the otter gives a physical advantage in encounters. Another factor is that otters are more selective in their diets, eating mainly fish. The mink are more versatile and eat many alternative foods and so can survive in areas well away from otters, without having to fight for disputed territory.

Mink nest in holes along river-banks, streams and lakes. The holes are usually under tree roots although they sometimes nest in hollow logs when they are found near to water. In view of the similar preferred habitat to the otter, it is not surprising that the former otter hunters turned their attention to the mink. Mink produce about five or six young in the spring, usually in May, and the female rears them until the autumn. Despite this, mink-hunting takes place in summer and in 1992 there were nineteen packs of hounds in England, Wales and Scotland. The mink emits a foul-smelling scent and hounds have little trouble in following it. As a result, the pursuit of the mink usually takes place over much shorter distances in much less time than the former otter-hunts. When cornered, the mink although normally silent, screams and spits in fury but hounds have little difficulty in killing it. Mink climb trees quite readily and have been known to do so to avoid the hounds.

Terriers accompany the hounds on mink-hunts and are used to locate and bolt the mink from refuges, such as holes in the ground, for the hounds to follow. If a terrier meets a mink on land it will normally readily kill it, despite the savage bite that its adversary can inflict. When swimming, the terrier is at a disadvantage should it encounter a mink. The terrier is often bitten on the face as it has to reach shallow water before it can effectively 'shake' the mink to destroy it. The hunting of mink has not only contributed to keeping packs of otter-hounds together but has also assisted, alongside trapping, in conserving a variety of native wildlife which, in all probability, would otherwise have been destroyed by the mink. The mink has proved to be a cunning and difficult animal to control and a determined escaper when captive.

Due to the effects on native wildlife, the Government in 1962 designated the mink as a dangerous pest and under the Destructive Imported Animals Act 1932 imposed restrictions on the keeping of mink. Later, the Mink Keeping Order 1972 strengthened the legislation, and strict security arrangements were introduced to minimize the risk of escapees from fur farms. Landowners who found mink on their land were required by law to notify the Ministry of Agriculture. The mink was then trapped and destroyed. The Ministry loaned special cages to use as traps and gave advice on the recommended procedures to destroy the mink. After trapping, the cage with the animal inside was placed in a sack, together with a wad of cotton wool soaked in the liquid halogenated hydrocarbon, carbon tetrachloride. The mouth of the sack was then sealed and the toxic fumes quickly anaesthetized and killed the mink. The original Mink Keeping Order 1972 has been updated several times and the current legislation is detailed in the Mink Keeping Order 1992.

9 Angling

The history of angling in England divides into two main themes. Firstly, the development of fishing-tackle through the centuries; and secondly, the social progression of the sport from the favoured few to the approximately three million anglers who fish in the United Kingdom today. Fishing is now one of man's principal relaxations. Angling comprises the art or skill of catching fish with rod, line and hook but this was not the usual method of fishing before the fifteenth century. It was then often done by net and spear to provide food without any hint of a sporting spirit. Most monasteries kept their own 'stew-ponds', where fish bred and a constantly renewed stock was maintained to be caught as required by the monks. Some religious establishments were conveniently sited alongside salmon streams for a similar reason.

The fifteenth century saw the beginnings of angling as a sport, as well as providing a welcome source of food. One of the earliest treatises on the subject was written as an appendix to the second edition of Dame Juliana Berners' book *The Boke of St Albans* in 1496. Wynkyn de Worde printed the work which was entitled *Treatyse of Fysshynge with an Angle*. It described the use of fishing rods about twenty feet long with lines of horsehair. The early use of artificial flies was also detailed. However, the most famous writer on freshwater angling was born about a century later in 1593. This was an Englishman, Izaak Walton, who wrote the well-known entertaining treatise on fishing in 1653 entitled *The Compleat Angler*, or 'The Contemplative Man's Recreation – Being a Discourse of Rivers Fishponds Fish and Fishing not unworthy of the Perusal of most Anglers'. The classic work has survived in print in many editions throughout the ensuing centuries and it is still read today. The book highlights the contentment and relaxation obtained from fishing in the near idyllic countryside alongside the English rivers of the seventeenth century. The six great rivers for fishing at the time were the Thames, Medway, Tweed, Severn, Tyne and Trent. One of his many amusing observations declares 'Doubt not therefore, Sir, but that Angling is an Art, and an Art worth your learning: the

Roach Fishing at Clewer Point on the Thames (*Edmund Bristow*)

question is rather, whether you be capable of learning it?'

A stained-glass window, called 'Study to be Quiet', now commemorates Izaak Walton in the Silkstede Chapel of Winchester Cathedral. It was donated by the fishermen of England in 1914 and shows Izaak Walton reading beside the River Itchen in Hampshire. His fishing-tackle lies beside him, with St Catherine's Hill in the background. Walton spent his later years at Winchester and died there at the age of ninety in 1683. Anglers also pay their respects to Izaak Walton by visiting a memorial museum to him at Shallowford, five miles to the north-east of Stafford. The museum is situated in a small thatched farm cottage which has unfortunately burned down twice this century. Each time it was painstakingly rebuilt and restored to recapture its original form. The cottage was bequeathed by Izaak Walton in the seventeenth century to the town of Stafford where he was born, so that the rent money yielded could be given to charitable purposes. The thatched cottage was originally a part of Izaak Walton's farm, although he himself was a successful ironmonger and tradesman in London who visited the countryside mainly for recreation. He had moved to London from Stafford at an early age to serve his apprenticeship in ironmongery with a relative.

The number of different species of freshwater fish found in the British Isles is relatively small, about thirty-eight. This is because the Ice Age made most waters uninhabitable to fish. Fortunately, many of the individual species which survive occur in large numbers, to the delight of anglers. The carp and rainbow trout were later introduced by man as a source of food, as well as for sport. The two prized game-fish have always been the salmon and trout, sought after in fast streams and rivers. The charr and grayling are their close relatives. However, the majority of people now angle for 'coarse fish' such as barbel, bream, carp, chub, dace, eels, gudgeon, pike, perch, roach and tench. The carp is a descendant of the fish formerly bred in the medieval monastic stew-ponds. Obviously, not every water is suitable for all these species, as some prefer fast-flowing streams whilst others thrive in more quiescent waters. In addition, some like gravel rather than mud on the bottom. Coarse fishing owes its enormous popularity to its ready accessibility and relatively low cost.

The angling which took place in the fifteenth and sixteenth centuries was mainly for carp, using a simple baited hook with a float and a line attached to a loop on the top of a wooden rod. The hooks and rods were homemade by the individual anglers in the fifteenth century but by the end of the sixteenth century, when angling as a sport became more popular, handmade rods and hooks could be purchased. Fishing-lines running along the rods, through guides, from reels were not used at the time, despite the knowledge of their existence in China for several centuries. In England, spare line was still wrapped around the hand in hanks or on a ring and cast from coils of line lying on the ground.

The floats favoured in the fifteenth and sixteenth centuries were either swans' quills or cork. It was recognized that a float was needed not only to support the weighted hook and bait but also to carry it to the fish through moving water. Additionally, the float indicated by bobbing when a 'bite' occurred. Swans quills were unobtrusive to the fish and at the same time reasonably visible to the angler. The baits were mainly worms, maggots and large insects. Fly-fishing was also attempted for trout by the more wealthy and it originally involved using a live fly. The art and skill was to lay it as lightly as possible on the surface of the water near the fish. As the sixteenth century progressed so different types and shapes of artificial flies were experimented with, as well as the natural insects.

The seventeenth century heralded the first design of a fish-hook based on more scientific principles than the earlier handmade ones. Charles Kirby, a needle-maker as well as a fish-hook manufacturer, invented a distinctive shape of hook in a tempered steel during the 1650s. The new shape eventually became known as the Kirby bend. The bend of the hook was slightly exaggerated from that of the normal round and the point and barb were turned slightly outwards. These modifications improved the chance of holding a fish once hooked. The wider curve of the bend at the weakest point reduced the tendency for the hook to open out when the fish fought against the tension. Charles Kirby and his associates worked from a shop in Shoe Lane, near Fleet Street, but the Great Plague of London and the Great Fire, during the period 1665 to 1666, caused them to leave their premises. Much later their factories were re-established in Redditch.

Many variations and specialist hooks have since been adapted from the Kirby but the basic principle has remained the same. Most hooks had a gut-eye to which the line was tied, although metal-eye hooks were invented in 1845 but did not become popular until around 1890. The twentieth century brought the development of the fully-closed hook-eye. This eliminated the risk of the line becoming trapped or damaged in the gap present in the former type of hook. Modern technology has also resulted in the production of extremely sharp hooks.

The fishing-lines used in the fifteenth and sixteenth centuries were as fine as practicable and made of twisted or plaited horsehair. The stronger the line required, the greater the number of hairs twisted together. The maximum feasible length of line made from horsehair was about three feet; therefore it was necessary to knot together a series of three-foot lengths to create a long length of line. Worsted silk was used to lash around each knot. Silk fishing-lines were also occasionally employed but they were prone to rot because a method of waterproofing them satisfactorily had not been discovered. Later in the seventeenth century, gut-strings and lute-strings made of glossy silk fabric were experimented with.

Throughout the eighteenth century and despite the introduction of an improved catgut which was thinner and stronger, horsehair still remained the favoured material for lines. Many preferred the hair obtained from the middle of the tail of a young grey stallion, as it was thought to be stronger. It was usual to make a tapered line of graduated thickness and it was often dyed to make it appear inconspicuous when in the water. The number of hairs twisted together was greatest (six or seven) at the point attached to the tip of the rod and the line decreased in diameter progressively until a single or perhaps two hairs were used to fasten the hook. Silkworm gut gained some popularity as an alternative line by the end of the

Fly-fishing (*William Jones*)

eighteenth century and it was later drawn through a die to produce a finer line. In the late 1870s, a heavy oiled line of silk came into fashion and was manufactured by coating the silk with oxidized linseed oil. The line was much easier to cast into the wind, although a stiffer rod was required. After casting, the oiled line floated. However, the silk line was left uncoated if it was required to sink in the water. These two alternative types of silk line gave an impetus to both dry and wet-fly angling. Previously it had been difficult to use horsehair lines for casting, as the knots joining the individual lengths were prone to catch on rod-rings and interfere with the smooth running of the line off a reel. Silk lines could be cast about three times as far.

In the late 1930s, the nylon monofilament line came into prominence but the outbreak of war prevented its wide usage until peace returned. Such a line offered many advantages, such as rot-resistance and strength, and it was hardly visible when attached to the hook. Nylon monofilament and the other synthetics which later developed, have low friction coefficients which made it much easier to cast the line. In fly-fishing, the 'fly' had virtually no weight and so the ability to cast from a reel depended solely on the weight of the line, as no float or lead was attached. Therefore a heavier line was used which was thicker in the middle of its length and tapered towards the end. This gave the necessary weight when the angler carried his rod back and then threw it forward to despatch the line into the water. The size of the line was matched to the particular rod.

Rod design was improved during the seventeenth century, and it became tapered. Different materials were spliced or joined together, the centre portion usually being made of bamboo cane, the top-end of whalebone and the butt-end of blackthorn. Most rods remained fairly stiff and were used more like poles as they were extremely long, of the order of sixteen feet or more. This allowed the hook and bait to be positioned accurately in the water far out from the river-bank. A long-length rod was necessary because the horsehair line was fixed to the end of it and was not cast. The majority of long rods were assembled from separate pieces by the use of brass sockets and ferrules to allow ease of carrying.

A large variety of woods were tried for rod manufacture throughout the eighteenth and nineteenth centuries, including willow and beech. In addition, butts were often made of crab-apple or ash and were sliced or jointed with a more flexible centre section of yew instead of the previously used whole cane. The upper, thinner section of the rod was still sometimes made of whalebone. The introduction of greenheart wood from South America and the West Indies saw the demise of the earlier mixtures of local woods by the turn of the nineteenth century. As well as greenheart, rods of hickory and lancewood were also manufactured, as these too were preferred, owing to their better elasticity, rather than the earlier heavier native woods.

Later in the nineteenth century, the use of rods known as 'split-cane' became even more popular for game-fishing than greenheart. The split-cane yielded a stiffer, shorter rod, possessing all the pliancy and strength of whole bamboo but with a reduced thickness. It was ideal to cast a line of oiled silk because by this time reels were being fitted to rods. The new rods were manufactured by splitting a bamboo cane, about two inches diameter, into sections which were then planed into suitable triangular shapes, so that they could be fitted accurately together and glued firmly. Normally, six triangular strips were laminated together to produce a hexagonal rod; a steel centre was sometimes incorporated. The overall design gave a soft-actioned rod, for use with a reel, which allowed the rod to bend throughout its length but with a gradual stiffening towards the butt-end. One of the greatest makers of rods at the end of the nineteenth century was the fishing-tackle company Hardy Brothers of Alnwick, Northumberland. The Hardy split-cane rods became synonymous with quality and were accepted as equals to those made by Charles Orvis and Hiram Leonard, the famous American rod manufacturers.

In contrast to the wealthier middle class who used split-cane rods, cheap bamboo rods, called roach poles, became extremely popular with many thousands of Victorian working-class anglers. The roach poles were made of natural whole bamboo and not of the expensive split-cane. They were fairly stiff and long and were made from telescopic sections of bamboo. There was no reel fitted. The line was simply tied at the tip of the rod and the line itself was about the length of the rod or sometimes shorter. When fishing, the rod was swung out gently over the water and the bait lowered carefully into a convenient free open stretch of water between the river reeds. When bringing in a hooked fish, the rod was simply shortened by removing the bottom joint lengths. The main catches were dace and roach. After fishing, the Victorian working-class angler coiled up his line by hand and carried his rod home, after dismantling into its individual lengths.

Many developments in rod materials and design have taken place this century. In the 1940s, hollow glass-fibre rods were introduced from the United States of America and offered advantages over split-cane ones on grounds of cost and reduced weight. The early designs of the long glass-fibre rods yielded tips which were too flexible but this problem was eventually alleviated by the calculation of the correct taper and the incorporation of various thicknesses of glass fibre. The glass-fibre rods have since been replaced by ones made of carbon fibre which are not only stronger but also even lighter. Boron rods have been introduced as well with some success,

Salmon Fishing
(*James Pollard*)

together with aramid fibre rods which allow very accurate casting due to their light, positive action.

The need for some form of device to take up and store long lengths of fishing-line on the rod became apparent in the seventeenth century. As a consequence, an unknown inventor attached a wire-ring at the tip of his rod and this allowed the passage of a running-line through it which could be cast and used to play a hooked fish. This led to the eventual invention of the English reel. With regard to its development, the late seventeenth century and the early eighteenth century saw the increasing use of a small brass winch, known as the multiplier. This was confined to the more wealthy who could afford to fish for salmon, and a few used it also for trout. The brass multiplier reel had a long axis and a small diameter but this early form of reel frequently jammed, especially when under load in salmon fishing. The principle of the multiplier was that it was geared and one turn of the handle (sometimes made of ivory) resulted in more than one revolution of the spool. This allowed the line to be recovered quickly when the fish ran towards the angler.

The unreliability of the multiplier reel under stress led to the development of an improved reel with a short axis and a large diameter. This was designed to allow braking of the line to prevent over-running when casting and to check the progress of a strong fish when hooked. The first reels of this type came into use in the second

half of the nineteenth century and at first they were confined mainly
to the Nottingham area of England. They were based on the local
technology acquired from the lacemaking industry's experience with
bobbins. The early form of Nottingham reel was made of wood and
the free-running, ungeared wide drum on a centre-pin was simply
checked during casting by the pressure of the angler's finger or
thumb. The reel was ideal to allow line and bait to float downstream
with the current. However, the reel had two main disadvantages.
Firstly, during casting a fairly heavy bait had to be used to overcome
the initial inertia of the reel and secondly, when reeling in quickly
with the handle on the side of the drum, the line often slipped off the
reel and became tangled. The tangle problem was made even worse
when later Nottingham reels were made of ebonite, a hard black
vulcanized rubber, or metal instead of wood. The change of material
improved further the free-running nature of the reel but
inadvertently increased the danger of tangling due to the increased
over-run.

Improvements were made to modify the reel and a line-guard was
fitted to prevent the line slipping off the reel. An adjustable device
was also employed to assist the angler in checking the line, without
purely relying on the pressure of his finger or thumb. The Malloch
reel, introduced in Scotland in 1880, allowed the spool to be moved
into two alternative positions, either parallel with the rod or at
right-angles to it. When casting, the parallel position was selected so
that the line could uncoil freely from the reel and through the rod
guides with less initial friction. When it was desired to wind the line
in, the spool was turned at right-angles to the rod. The major
disadvantage of the Malloch reel was that it was prone to twist the
line when reeling-in and this often led again to tangling. The Malloch
reel was mainly used when fishing for salmon.

The tangling problem was eventually overcome by the invention of
the fixed spool reel which became well established by the 1920s. The
basic principle of its mechanism was similar to that utilized for
cotton bobbins in the textile industry. The creative adaptation was
conceived by A.H. Illingworth in 1905, after studying various mills in
Lancashire. He worked in the textile industry himself. In the
fixed-spool reel, the spool was set at right-angles to the axis of the
rod. A major advantage over the earlier centre-pin reel was that in
long-distance casting the line was pulled freely from the spool.
Additionally, during winding-in, a pick-up arm automatically
rotated, spreading the line evenly on the spool to prevent tangling.
The spool itself did not turn when the line was being recovered. The
line was of a very light material, such as silk. To prevent line
breakage under stress a slipping clutch arrangement was incorporated to feed out automatically extra line when the loading, such

as playing a fish, demanded it.

The Hardy Brothers fishing-tackle company in Northumberland later gained a renowned reputation for the manufacture of its reels which were fitted to their equally famous rods. The reels, known as Hardy Perfects, were produced up to 1967. The very early models were usually stamped with an identifying number of the individual craftsman who constructed them. These numbered rods were made before the days of mass production. In the past two decades there has been a revolution in fixed-spool reel design, mainly due to the introduction of new materials, such as graphite composites, to reduce reel weight. In addition, these composites offer the advantage of being resistant to corrosion. Many sophisticated improvements have been made to the mechanics of reel systems as well, to allow the angler better control over his line.

In the seventeenth century, fishing for pleasure by the wealthy brought about the building of architect-designed fishing pavilions on several English estates. These little gazebos overlooked the river or lake and were constructed often in the Chinese style. Their numbers greatly increased in the eighteenth century and a royal pavilion was built during the next century by George IV in Windsor Great Park, overlooking Virginia Water. The eighteenth century brought an increase in the popularity of fishing for salmon and trout but the oppressive game laws limited it to the favoured few estate owners and those who could afford the high costs of fishing rights and rents. These became even more expensive by the end of the eighteenth century and it cost in excess of one hundred pounds to fish the best chalk streams, such as the Itchen and Test. Many Victorian tradesmen, who had become fairly prosperous, took up angling with their split-cane rods, mainly perhaps because they thought it socially advantageous to take part in some form of field sport. They could not quite afford to participate regularly in fox-hunting, so they stood on the river-banks with their fishing-rods. In order to prove they were not working-class, many would dress elaborately with their best tailored waistcoats beneath their velvet jackets. Colourful trousers and a top hat would be proudly worn as they fished. A century before, the fashionable fishing coat was black or a dark colour and the hat worn was a black velvet cap, similar to a large jockey's cap. The Victorian angler would have his landing net by his side to assist him when a catch was made. Such nets were often made with a hoop of brass to support a corded net. A telescopic cane handle was attached to the brass, so that a section could be detached and the length shortened as required.

With regard to early angling for trout and salmon, Robert Venables, a colonel in Cromwell's army, laid the foundations for seventeenth-century trout and salmon fly-fishing, although a

Fishing on the Avon, Fordingbridge (*Henry Alken, Sen.*)

gentleman called Foster was probably the first to use the dry or floating fly for trout in Derbyshire's rivers. Colonel Venables wrote *The Experienc'd Angler* in 1662 and later helped to produce the fifth edition of *The Compleat Angler*, together with Charles Cotton, a Staffordshire gentleman writer. The earlier anglers for salmon preferred to use a baited hook rather than a fly, as their lines were made of horsehair and difficult to cast. Likewise for trout, a natural fly could also not easily be cast and anglers used insects, such as mayflies or grasshoppers, on their hooks, which they lowered carefully into the river with their long rods.

In the following century, artificial flies imitating natural ones came more into use and for catching salmon it became normal to utilize a wet fly that was sunk either deep or just below the surface of the water. It is surprising that salmon can be caught using either baits or artificial flies because they enter the fresh waters of rivers to spawn and not to feed. The spawning takes place from November to February. Perhaps they take a bite at a fly solely out of irritation. With experience it was found that the salmon shied away from too gaudy a fly and in clear water a dark fly was more successful. However, when the water was murky a bright fly was vital to attract the salmon's attention. Nowadays, the type and size of fly used for salmon fishing depends on the depth of the water and temperature. A huge variety is available.

During the eighteenth and nineteenth centuries, few English anglers had the opportunity to fish for salmon, unless they were wealthy and were prepared to travel by the available transport of the day to the salmon rivers, mainly in the north of the British Isles, Wales and Ireland. It is thought that the last salmon was caught in the River Thames in 1821 but prior to this date salmon from the Thames sold at a high price on the London market, as it was fresher and thought better tasting than salmon brought to the city from the north or other rivers. In the nineteenth century, royalty started to use the Highland rivers and Scotland became fashionable with rich English sportsmen. They were accompanied by the ghillie of the estate to advise on the local fishing. A ghillie was originally the male servant of a Highland chieftain but the meaning became widened to denote the attendant of a sportsman. Today, salmon fishing remains beyond the reach of most people, again because of the expense; fishing in the waters of the Highlands can cost in the region of a thousand pounds a week.

Some of the very rich Victorian sportsmen of England in the late nineteenth century even undertook the tedious journey to Norway to fish for the bigger salmon to be found in the larger and faster-flowing rivers. They wielded extremely long greenheart rods, fitted with massive reels especially made by Hardy, to land the heavy and powerful Norwegian salmon. The leaping salmon on its way upstream to its spawning grounds was considered the prime and most elusive quarry for the Victorian sportsman. This so-called king of fish presented an exciting challenge, as they often eluded the hook or broke the line to make good their escape. This was in contrast to trout and coarse fish which, when hooked, were generally landed. Even when hooked, the salmon ran and leapt and had to be skilfully played to bring it to the river-bank. The Victorians developed a wide variety of elaborate salmon flies to lure the salmon; the wet fly was still found much more successful than the dry. The flies were of different sizes and shapes; some were single hooks and others double hooks. The hooks were dressed with feathers, fur, wool, silk, etc and fashioned to a shape which imitated a natural fly at some stage of its development. The type of fly selected depended upon the conditions when fishing and they were carried in a wallet or tin to prevent them being crushed. In another container would be a number of instruments to assist the tying of the fly to the line. These would include a small vice for holding the hook, a special needle secured to a wooden handle to prick out the eye of the hook, and a pair of forceps.

The anglers wore fashionable waders when fishing and on the river-bank were assembled essential items of their equipment. These included a creel, often made of expensive split reed bound in leather, for storing their fish or spare tackle. Near at hand was a salmon gaff, with a sturdy brass hook securely fastened to a rosewood handle. This was used to assist the landing of a large fish. If the angler was of an optimistic nature there may also have been a brass scale to weigh his salmon. When anglers were unsuccessful using a wet fly for salmon, they often turned to spinning or bait fishing with an artificial lure. Spinning was usually performed when there was a high river level and the water was cold. The technique allowed fishing at a deeper depth than with a wet fly. In the eighteenth century, the spinning baits were small fish on multi-hooked flights with bent tails to impart the required spin. An improvement came in the nineteenth century when a toothed-jaw mechanism held the bait and this was attached to two small propellers to obtain the spin or rotation. Later, an artificial bait in the shape of a fish and known as the 'Devon minnow' came into prominence. This was available in various sizes and colours, with vanes to make it spin against the pressure of the river current. They were made of wood or metal and fitted with a treble hook. Nowadays, plastic vanes are fitted to impart the spin. There were many other types of spinner, and metal 'spoons' with a wobbling action instead of spin were also used. The fishing rods for spinning were shorter (about nine feet) than those for fly-fishing (over twelve feet). As a consequence, the former were usually in two pieces while the latter were constructed in three sections. Both were generally used double-handed by the angler.

When angling for trout, both wet and dry flies are now employed and most anglers use short cane rods of between six and eight feet; the rods are always held single-handed. In wet-fly fishing, more than one fly may be attached to the sunken length of cast. However, in dry-fly fishing only a single fly is used and when cast floats freely, the movement attracting the attention of the trout. In general terms, wet flies are preferred for streams running over peat and dry flies for spring-fed streams running over chalk, such as those in Hampshire and Wiltshire. The peaty streams possess some acidity, whilst the chalky ones are on the alkaline side. The chalky streams provide a better environment for floating aquatic insects and the trout mistakes an imitation fly on the surface for its natural food. However, it was not until the period 1860 to 1870 that dry flies were widely used. Earlier, Alfred Ronalds had conducted a scientific study into the types of flies and aquatic insects the trout favoured for food. The results of his work were published during 1836 in his book *The Fly Fisher's Entomology*. This led to the improved imitation of natural insects and artificial flies.

Until the middle of this century, the quarry was the wild brown trout found in our fast-flowing rivers and streams. However, the price of fishing rights for the favoured chalk streams became very high and the second half of the century saw the stocking of reservoirs, flooded disused quarries and gravel pits with rainbow trout. This species of trout was first introduced from the west-coast rivers of the United States of America. This revolutionized traditional fly-fishing and 'fancy flies' and 'lures', previously experimented with in the eighteenth and nineteenth centuries for trout, but rarely used, became popular for reservoir fishing. The fancy flies were much gaudier and larger than imitation flies and bore a closer resemblance to a small fish than a natural fly. They were somewhat similar to the artificial lures used for salmon. In order to cast the line further into the wide expanse of still water of a reservoir, a longer, stiffer rod was preferred to that used for traditional river trout fishing. In addition, anglers sometimes spin for trout and favour a light two-piece rod, around seven feet long, with a fixed spool-reel. Anglers value the rainbow trout because it grows very quickly in comparison to the

Pike Fishing (*Newton Fielding*)

native brown trout. Also, there is no statutory close season for
rainbow trout, although sometimes there are local by-laws imposing
one.

The cost of fishing for salmon and river trout has continued to deter
many and led them to take up coarse fishing. In this type of fishing
the quarry is not caught for food (as most are not good to eat) but
purely for sport, and the fish is usually carefully returned to the
water after capture with little harm. This is done always by handling
the fish with wet hands and holding it in the water facing upstream
until it swims free; sometimes barbless hooks are used. The fishing is
done purely for sport with either a float, ledger or paternoster.
Sometimes combinations of these are used; all these techniques were
known as long ago as the seventeenth century.

When a float was used for coarse fishing, lead shot sank the bait
down to the fish. The size of shot was matched to suit the type and
design of the float. Different types were used depending on whether
the river was relatively still, or fast flowing. During the eighteenth
century, a tiny bell fixed on the end of the rod or attached to the float
signalled a 'bite'. Anglers now use alternative materials to lead shot
for weights; the sale of sizes between No. 8 and No. 15 was banned at
the end of 1986. This came about as a result of lost or discarded small
lead shot causing the choking or poisoning of many swans and other
aquatic wildlife.

Many anglers thought that the movement, resistance and drag of a
float discouraged fish such as carp to bite, and they preferred
so-called free-line fishing or ledgering. In this, a float was omitted
and special weights, such as the pear-shaped Arlesey bomb, were
used to sink the bait to the bottom and allowed it to be fished without
movement. A mark just above the reel gave warning of a 'bite' or
alternatively the end of the rod was carefully watched. A light line
was used and the rod placed in rod-rests to allow the line to run freely
off the spool when a bite occurred. Instead of ledgering, another
method employed for coarse fishing was the paternoster. In this
technique, the tackle was usually weighted to the bed of the river or
lake and live bait used to entice the quarry. There was a tight line to
the rod and the baits were held on several hook lengths attached to
fixed wire booms positioned at right-angles to the suspended tackle.
Alternatively, especially on lakes, the tackle was not weighted to the
bed but allowed to float on the surface, the buoyancy being achieved
by small blocks of wood spaced at intervals. The hook lengths were
suspended down from the floating blocks by weights placed at
intervals along the lines.

Individual techniques and tackles were favoured for different
species of coarse fish. The coarse fish were usually taken with natural
baits such as maggots, worms or small fish. Anglers later used

artificial flies as well, together with spinning baits and plugs. The latter type of lure did not rotate like the spinner but instead dived and darted through the water. There were two general types of plug, known as sinkers and floaters. They were mainly kept for pike fishing and the plugs had plates fitted to their nose ends so that the winding-in of the line caused them to dive in the water.

In the industrial areas of the Midlands and north of England during the latter part of the nineteenth century, the wealthier middle classes anxious for sporting pleasure and status would travel to their nearest rivers for trout and salmon. The industrialists from Birmingham would fish the River Severn, those from Sheffield the waters of the Peak District, and those from Lancashire the large expanses of water in the Lake District. The cost of fishing rights in the favoured waters doubled in the period 1880 to 1890. Rod licences were also introduced during the 1870s in an attempt to preserve the stocks of game-fish. There had been much over-fishing. The cost involved was well beyond the English working class and they chose coarse fishing which was open to all, as no rod licence was required for this sport. In fact, rod licences for coarse fishing were not introduced into England until the 1960s. The English working man was unlucky in one respect because his counterparts in Ireland, Scotland and Wales could indulge in trout fishing as there were plentiful supplies in their local rivers and streams.

Many thousands of working-class anglers living in the industrialized areas of northern England organized trips to the nearby countryside to pursue their hobby of coarse fishing. Unfortunately, most of the streams and rivers in their localities were heavily polluted and the fish were relatively poor specimens and sparse. In order to make their sport more exciting, competitions between individuals were arranged and inevitably betting on the results took place. Public houses and working-men's clubs also began to run competitions on a local team and club basis; sweepstakes were held with the winner taking all the pooled money, plus any winning side bets struck. Later, cups, medals and other prizes were competed for which led to large matches with hundreds of anglers taking part along the same stretch of river. The exact position for each angler on the river-bank was determined by a draw before the event started and the individual places marked with pegs. Sheffield became an important centre for such activities and when they expanded beyond local club competitions, The Angling Association was founded in 1869. During the late Victorian period, many coarse fishermen pressed their Members of Parliament to lobby for a close season to protect their fish supplies, especially in the fish spawning season when it was desirable to leave the waters in peace. The close season for coarse fishing became the middle of March to the middle of June.

By the turn of the nineteenth century, nearly every public house in the north of England had an angling club and even in London the pubs claimed over six hundred different ones. Railway day excursions were organized which gave speedier access to countryside waters. Due to the nationwide popularity of competitions, The National Federation of Anglers was formed in 1903, which ran the National Championships each year, the first being held in 1906 on the River Thames with seven teams taking part. As well as the National Championships, divisional competitions took place at selected venues around England. Later, fishing-tackle manufacturers started to sponsor some of the championship events and offered substantial prize money. It was clear that the working man favoured competitive fishing, in contrast to the wealthier members of society who mainly fished for a more leisurely pleasure.

The outbreak of the First World War caused the demise of most forms of competitive and pleasure fishing. However, the end of the war did not bring a revival in pub club fishing because many anglers

Pike Fishing on the River Lea (*James Pollard*)

preferred to join the many company fishing clubs that were being formed. The miners in the north of England fished with their social clubs and betting always remained an integral part of the day's fun. Anglers have always loved to claim they had caught a very large fish and this led to a type of fishing known as specimen hunting. It was especially popular in the 1950s and the specimen hunter usually sought only his favourite species which may have been roach, carp or barbel depending upon the angler's preference. Equally, anglers also liked to talk about the one that got away but as Izaak Walton once said, 'No man can lose what he never had'! In the early 1960s, a gentleman named Eric Hudson founded the National Association of Specimen Groups to represent the interests of specimen hunters around the country. It later changed its name to the National Association of Specialist Anglers.

In the later 1960s a change took place and anglers, in competition, thought that the total combined weight of fish caught was much more important than the size of individual fish. The total catch landed by each angler was therefore weighed en masse before the fish were released back alive into the water. This non-killing policy was also pursued by fishermen who angled only for leisurely pleasure. There were many of these who set off in their cars for a day's fishing in their local river or in a stocked flooded gravel pit or reservoir. As well as the fishing, they enjoyed the solitude and peace which could not be found in competitive fishing. They could also move about as they were not tied to an allocated spot as in competitive angling.

All anglers who fish need a rod licence and the fees charged provide nearly a half of the total funds required by the National Rivers Authority for their various fishery schemes. These include such matters as the prevention of river pollution, the control of fishing to restrict exploitation of stocks, and the monitoring and maintenance of fish hatcheries to provide better fishing for the angler. The Government contributes the remaining money needed by means of a grant. The National Rivers Authority was formed in the autumn of 1989, when the old water authorities became regions of the new central authority. The National Rivers Authority rationalized the whole rod licence system in 1992 by issuing a single all-species national licence to cover English and Welsh waters. The following year the annual rod licence fee was set at £13.25 but in addition a new short-term licence was introduced for the occasional angler. This cost £6.75 for a seven-day period. There was a concessionary annual licence for juniors aged twelve to sixteen years, the disabled and the over sixty's at £6.75. The licences were mainly purchased from about 2000 agents nationwide, most of whom were fishing-tackle shops. They were also bought direct from the National Rivers Authority's regional offices. However, already the question of whether to proceed with a single-tier rod licence is under review. The National Rivers Authority may change to a three-tier system of charging coarse-fish anglers £15 per year, trout anglers £22.50 per year and salmon anglers £75 per year for their rod licences. Much depends upon the levels of future government grants.

The rod licence enables the angler to use a rod and line but this does not in itself confer a right to fish. Fishing in 'inland waters' is private and therefore it can only take place if the prospective angler obtains permission to fish from the riparian owner or his representative. This may necessitate him joining an angling club to fish their waters or purchasing a day ticket for a permit. Most fisheries impose a 'limit bag' which specifies the total number of fish which may be caught with a single ticket. Some limit the number of anglers. Anyone who trespasses, catches and takes fish away without permission commits an offence under the Theft Act 1968.

The large number of people who now enjoy angling imposes an increasing pressure on the wild fish stocks in rivers and it is often necessary to undertake regular stocking to supplement the natural populations of wild fish. The same precedent applies, of course, to the still-water fisheries in reservoirs and flooded gravel pits. During the first few weeks after stocking the fish are easier to catch than the native fish because they are less wary. In the hatchery they have become accustomed to feeding exclusively on the surface. Fortunately, anglers keep a vigilant eye on pollution in our rivers and report it to the relevant regional river authority when discovered. The authorities investigate all complaints of pollution and take appropriate action against the offenders when they are traced. The improving quality of river water has not only been beneficial to the fish but has helped the waterbird and fowl population, such as kingfishers, moorhens and mute swans, to increase again.

10   Poaching, Forest and Game Laws

The early feudal system of England ensured that each lord of the manor owned a mixture of arable, pasture and open uncultivated land. The cottagers, or commoners as they were later called, were granted rights of common, such as the grazing of animals on the lord's open uncultivated land. There were several other rights, including that of collecting small branches and brushwood for fuel and the taking of fish from lakes and streams. Poaching in England began in earnest when much of this former land allowed for common use, together with the wild birds, fish and animals on it, became exclusively reserved for the use and pleasure of a privileged few.

The Norman Conquest of England accelerated poaching because following the Conquest, very large tracts of land were seized and added to the already vast areas of royal forests, established by the Saxons. Many of the ancient rights and privileges were abolished by the Normans. The poachers were local poor people who strove to fill the empty bellies of their families. As the poaching was done to procure food, the poacher felt no guilt in stealing the king's deer or trespassing on a rich landowner's property, especially when the land was reserved purely for the sport of venery or hunting. Even members of the clergy thought it tolerable for a man living in poverty to catch game on a rich man's land.

In medieval times, most poachers hunted their quarry with large nets or bows and arrows. They stretched the nets across trees to entangle deer as they ran, or slung a series of ropes at strategic levels between the boughs to ensnare the antlers of the running deer. The deer were driven by the poachers into the nets or ropes, and such traps became known as 'buckstalls'. As well as procuring food, the act of poaching gave the men a sense of excitement and bravado which enlivened their humdrum existence. They were confident in the knowledge that their neighbours would be unwilling to betray them to the keepers of the royal forests.

Convicted poachers through the centuries have suffered penalties ranging from death, blinding, castration, maiming, imprisonment and transportation to fines. Punishment started with the introduc-

tion of the Forest Laws in Norman times, which sacrificed the interests and rights of nearly all the people of England, so that the king had an abundance of game to hunt for his sport. The potential penalties for infringing the Forest Laws were harsh. It is difficult to establish how frequently the severest sentences of death or mutilation were imposed because alternative punishments of imprisonment and heavy fines were also available for offenders. The management of a royal forest was the responsibility of the Lord Warden, or Keeper, who was usually a man of high birth and social status. Under him were a host of officials, such as verderers, foresters, rangers, beadles and under-keepers. Their main responsibility was the practical husbandry of the forest rather than the apprehension of miscreants such as poachers.

The Forest Law deemed that all cottagers living within the royal forests could only lawfully possess weapons if they were fitted with blunt arrowheads. This was to ensure that the deer were reserved solely for the king. In addition, all dogs in the royal forests had to be 'humbled' or 'lawed' so that they could not harm the deer. These cruel practices involved mutilating the dogs to reduce their speed. 'Humbling', as it was called, was probably first introduced in Saxon times during the reign of Edward the Confessor, and it consisted of severing the back sinews of the dogs' hind legs. During Norman times, the method was replaced by 'lawing', which involved laming the dogs by cruelly placing their front paws on a block of wood and chopping off three claws from each, with a mallet or hammer and chisel. Small dogs were exempted from the treatment if they could crawl successfully through an iron stirrup which was used to gauge their size. Different-size stirrups were used in the various royal forests but an example of the type favoured in the New Forest in Hampshire may still be viewed in the Verderers Hall at Lyndhurst.

One benefit to come from the Forest Laws was that the wildlife prospered, as land was no longer put to the plough and the game was protected from the vast majority of the population. For example, the wild boar survived, possibly as long as the seventeenth century, because it was reserved exclusively by the Forest Laws for hunting. Otherwise the wild boar would probably have become extinct a century or so earlier, as the animals were both dangerous to man and destructive to crops. The boar's head was considered a delicacy for a banquet but the hunting of them in the forest entailed grave risks to men, horses and hounds. In view of this, all three wore body armour but despite the protection many hounds in particular died in their encounters with the wild boars. The hounds favoured for the task were the large mastiffs or alaunts who hunted both by scent and sight. They were so savage that most were kept muzzled until they were released for hunting. When the boar was held at bay by the

A Poacher Surprised
(*William Jones*)

mastiffs, the men attacked their quarry simultaneously with their swords and spears. King Henry I and King John were both keen hunters of the boar.

The Norman kings occasionally gave some of their subjects the right to hunt wild animals which were considered harmful to the so-called beasts of the chase. These included the wolf, the wild cat and the fox, all considered enemies of the countryside. The wolf was a significant predator of deer. Wildfowl were at first not protected by the Forest Laws but people still faced the harsh penalties for trespass if they were caught on the king's land. For this reason, many of the poor people netted and snared wildfowl in the estuaries away from the royal forests.

The original afforestation concept created by William I was broadened by Henry I and then by Henry II in the twelfth century, with the development of special courts to punish offenders under the Forest Laws. During their reigns and the succeeding reigns of Richard I and King John, the clergy were only subject to Ecclesiastic Law and not bound by the restrictive practices of other laws. In theory, they could hunt and possess hawks in a similar manner to knights and barons, but King John resisted this, probably because too much of his game was being taken. In addition, he sanctioned a proclamation in 1209 which disallowed the taking of wildfowl, by any means, in England. Again, this was probably due to his avaricious nature, believing he was being deprived of future prey for his falcons.

King John had many quarrels with the Church and he was excommunicated in 1209. Many powerful people conspired to obtain a return of their liberties and protested against his hated government. These objections against King John eventually led to the passing of the Magna Carta in 1215 which reinstated the rights of the Church, the barons and all in the land. One of the minor consequences was the deforestation of land previously seized by King John, and the banning of many of his detested laws. It allowed the barons to secure their own right to hunt and this was termed 'granting rights of warren'. Later, stretches of forest with hunting rights were granted to individuals as private forests, and these were called 'chases'. The word 'chase' derived from the Norman French, *chace* meaning 'hunt'. Offenders of the laws caught in a warren or chase were tried under the jurisdiction of the Common Law, instead of the Forest Law.

The Carta de Foresta was introduced in 1225 by Henry III and was the first charter to deal exclusively with the forests. It decreased still further the game rights in the control of the Crown, and allowed the clergy to participate more freely in hunting. A clause allowed an archbishop, a bishop, an earl or a baron, when passing through a royal forest, to kill one deer, as long as a horn was first blown to warn the forestor. The Carta de Foresta also abolished capital punishment and mutilation for offences against the royal preserves and the Forest Law.

The ratification of the Confirmatio Cartarum, by Edward I in 1327, prevented the king imposing taxes at will, without due assent of his barons, and halted forcible seizures of land and property. It also led to a decline in the enforcement of the Forest Law, other than the imposition of fines. As a consequence, many keepers of the royal forests started to use their own 'club' law instead, meting out punishment with their cudgels on the heads of trespassers and poachers. However, it took many years before the complete concept of Forest Law was abandoned and although the powers were rarely used, it survived until 1817.

Alongside the Forest Law was the Common Law, by which all things belonged to the Crown unless someone else could claim right of property. This applied not only to inanimate objects and materials but also to animals in the wild, such as deer and game. Common Law was unwritten and based on customs and usage which had become common throughout England. It was not passed by legislation and it became firmly established by the thirteenth century. It was based on the principle of judicial precedent which meant that earlier decisions or judgements were binding in considering a similar case. Common Law allowed the Crown to pass its rights to others by grant, if it so desired. By this means, Edward III in 1377 gave landowners with a certain income the right to take game. Later, this precedent eventually formed the basis of drafting the English Game Laws during the seventeenth and later centuries. However, the penalties for infringing the early Game Laws became nearly as severe as those of the Forest Laws. In Edward III's reign, the theft of a hawk trained for falconry was punishable by death. The offence of finding a hawk and not informing the Sheriff of the County resulted in two years' imprisonment.

Following Edward III's granting of rights to take game, a statute was passed in 1389 during Richard II's reign which stipulated the law in more detail. The right was limited to persons with estates yielding more than forty shillings income a year, plus clerks with an income of ten pounds per annum. However, the game had to be taken only with the aid of hounds, ferrets and snares; no other method was allowable. Eventually the right to take game became incidental to the ownership of land. Just over a century later, Henry VII took positive action to ensure that hunting was restricted to the landowners and the more wealthy by the passing of another statute. This prevented the common people from owning dogs, ferrets, guns, nets, snares or any equipment which could be used in the pursuit of bird or beast. It also decreed that anyone convicted of stealing a young hawk or eggs from a nest would be imprisoned for one year and one day. A beneficial outcome was that this early form of conservation law helped considerably to increase the native population of hawks in England. Elizabeth I later reduced the sentence to three months' imprisonment.

When Henry VIII succeeded his father, a statute was passed in 1534 to restrict the taking and destruction of wildfowl and their eggs. It imposed a close season from the end of May to the last day of August. The only people allowed to take wildfowl in the permitted season were certain freeholders, and they had to hunt them solely with the use of longbows and spaniels. To enforce this, it became an offence for anyone except those who owned land to the value of a hundred pounds per annum, to keep in their homes crossbows or any early form of gun. The punishment for an offence under the law was a

Freeman, The Earl of Clarendon's Game-keeper, with a Dying Doe and a Hound (*George Stubbs*)

fine of ten pounds. Although wildfowl were not classified as game-birds, a close season has been maintained ever since Henry VIII's edict. However, the precise dates have changed many times. From the nineteenth century onwards, a series of Wild Birds Protection Acts have stipulated the close seasons, together with the penalties for infringing them. The general close season is now 1st February to 31st August inclusive, but there are variations depending upon the particular species of wildfowl.

At the beginning of the seventeenth century, during James I's reign, an Act was passed which further reserved game for the more wealthy members of the community. This prohibited a person from taking any kind of game, if he was of the so-called 'vulgar sort' or of 'small worth'. The penalty for an offender was a heavy fine or, in default of payment, imprisonment with hard labour ranging from ten days to one month, plus a whipping to be administered in prison. Another statute was passed by Charles II's Cavalier Parliament in 1671 which defined in greater detail the type of person entitled to take game. It was restricted to the small minority who owned large freehold estates worth at least a hundred pounds a year and those with leasehold estates of one hundred and fifty pounds per annum.

In reality, this prevented the vast majority of landowners from taking game even on their own land. As a result many took to the use of the snare and net. In effect, they became poachers on their own land. The penalty for infringing the 1671 Act was a fine of five pounds or imprisonment for three months. This Act was to survive for one and a half centuries and its effect fostered great antagonism between the classes. However, an important outcome of the law was that the Crown had acknowledged in effect that it no longer had an exclusive right to all game, as some of its rights were being passed to the wealthier landowners. This set the pattern that the ownership of land gave power and formed the best title to claim property of game.

The theme continued throughout the Restoration period, when the early Game Laws were drafted to ensure that the powerful squirearchy of England had plenty of partridges and salmon to shoot and catch. Even at the beginning of the twentieth century, there appeared to be an alliance between the aristocrats and squires against the rest of the working rural community, who viewed a little poaching as harmless. The squire often sat on the Bench in the court which punished the wrong-doer who had been caught helping himself to his pheasants. The seventeenth and eighteenth centuries saw the start of commercial poaching, and most of the game on the London markets came from this source. The majority of the illicit game found its way to London through the connivance of stagecoach drivers, mail transport guards and other men travelling on regular horse-drawn waggons. The ordinary people, unlike the landowners, were sympathetic to poachers, as they had always been to smugglers.

By the nineteenth century, poaching became even more of a sport, as well as a welcome means of food procurement. It hinted at a covert method of carrying out a type of class warfare against the local squire, and a favourite way to antagonize a particularly unpopular one was to steal his pheasant and partridge eggs. Many thought that the game found in the woods and fields ought to be free to everyone and the villagers accepted the poacher as a part of their community. They never considered him a criminal carrying out an act of trespass and stealing, although at the time poaching carried a possible penalty of imprisonment or transportation to the colonies. They would often be pleased to get a hare, pheasant or salmon from him and reward him with a few drinks at the inn. The gamekeeper rarely visited the inn because the villagers would then know his whereabouts and the poacher with his companions would be free to proceed safely with their unlawful mission. The gamekeeper therefore led a fairly solitary existence. Despite this, the village poacher made it his business to know when the gamekeeper returned to his cottage at night. He could then go out safely wearing his huge sagging coat, with its large pockets, to conceal his anticipated haul of game stolen from the squire. Most poachers were reluctant to take their dogs with them because they might bark.

The further establishment of private land for deer stalking, hare coursing, salmon fishing and pheasant shooting during the eighteenth and nineteenth centuries necessitated the employment of many more gamekeepers and water bailiffs to protect the game. In the eighteenth century, some of the gamekeepers could almost be accused of being poachers themselves, as they often kept and sold game for their own use. In the nineteenth century, poaching assumed an even more commercial outlook than in the previous century. The solitary village poacher still remained, but as the Game Laws became more severe, whole gangs started to invade the countryside from the industrial towns. Many bloody battles were to ensue with the gamekeepers.

At night, the gamekeepers carried lanterns which they lit suddenly to catch a brief glimpse of a poacher's face, so that he could be identified later. If the gamekeeper recognized a familiar face, he would never shout his name. Many poachers thought it better to murder a gamekeeper than to be identified in Court in the future, and at least forty-two gamekeepers were killed in the period 1833 to 1843. In spite of the danger, many poachers were caught and about one in fourteen of all convicted criminals were poachers. During 1844, 4279 game convictions were recorded in England; most were for the poaching of rabbits and pheasants.

Vigilance was the main weapon of the gamekeepers but various contraptions and 'engines', as they were called at the time, were devised to help them catch the poachers. These included alarm-sticks, man-traps and spring guns. As a consequence, the poachers when trying to snare game had to be wary not to be trapped themselves. The alarm-stick was used mainly to scare the poachers away and to warn the gamekeepers that they were in the vicinity. Such a device consisted of an iron stick driven into the ground; the base of the stick had a recess to attach a firing-pin with a blank cartridge above. This was rigged, via a simple mechanism, to a trip-wire. When the trip-wire was pulled, it extracted a holding pin which caused the blank cartridge to be driven down onto the firing-pin with a resulting loud percussion bang. The gamekeepers would then immediately move into the area to search for the poachers, but most would have vanished by the time they arrived.

Far more cruel were the man-traps hidden in the undergrowth. These were designed to maim rather than kill, and took the form of huge gin-traps. There were several varieties, including toothless, half-toothed and bruisers. All forms had a treading-plate fixed in the middle of the large open jaws of the trap, which when trodden on caused the jaws to snap shut on the unfortunate poacher's leg. The trap held him until the gamekeeper arrived. The toothless type inflicted severe pain and flesh bruising. The half-toothed variety was more severe, as it had two-inch teeth of various curvatures and shapes designed to cause bruising and laceration of the soft tissue and to restrain the victim in agony. The third type, the bruiser, was designed to crush the bone of the leg of the trapped victim.

Although such traps could maim a man for life, they were unlikely to kill him. Far more deadly was the spring-gun which, when triggered by a concealed trip-wire, fired a ball or shot. These were much used around 1815. As well as poachers, innocent people stumbled across the hidden devices and they were just as likely to be killed as the poacher. As a consequence, the use of such engines was banned by an Act of Parliament in 1827. Anyone found setting spring-guns or man-traps with intent to endanger life was liable to be imprisoned for a period of up to five years.

For catching rabbits in the nineteenth century, the poacher's favourite method was to use a ferret, which was sent down the burrow, with purse nets pegged over the exits. The ferrets were carried muzzled in special boxes or bags by the poacher. He fitted bells to his ferrets, so that they could be more readily found after release. Snares and gin-traps were also set to catch rabbits and these were extremely cruel, as they locked onto the rabbit's leg without killing it outright. Such traps are now illegal and only special small spring-traps approved by the Ministry of Agriculture, which kill instantly, may be utilized. They are set in the runs and covered with earth to hide their presence. A special spade is used to dig out a space for the tread-plate which must be placed inside the mouth of the rabbit burrow, under the overhang, to prevent other animals being trapped and possibly killed. Such traps must be inspected regularly by the farmer or gamekeeper. Nowadays, poachers are no longer very interested in rabbits or the legal small spring-trap. They prefer to poach the more valuable deer or salmon.

Snares were also set by poachers to trap pheasants. A gang of experienced men could lay more than a hundred snares in a short space of time. They would then retreat and return later, walking in a line to collect their illicit bag. Partridges were more difficult to catch, and a favourite method for the solitary poacher was to peg into the ground a series of loop-snares made from horsehair. These were set at night near the favoured territory of the partridges. The large-scale poaching gangs caught their partridges by first disturbing them at dusk, to note where they rested on the ground, and later returning to drag nets over them after they had settled down again for the night. This method was only practicable when the resting ground was clear of hedges and other obstacles which were likely to snag the net during the procedure. The net was large, up to twenty yards long, with weights tied to one side of it. Two to four men handled the net, depending on its size; any more would have caused too much noise. The net was held taut and high when the men stealthily approached the partridges. It was then slowly lowered, as the partridges were approached, before the final throw to entangle them. The venture was not always successful as the partridges often rose before the net fell.

One method of poaching hares at night was to drape a net over a farm-gate in a field where hares were likely to be. The net was approximately the same size as the gate and was held in position by the weight of several large stones placed on top of it along the upper bar. A line of stones were also placed on the bottom of the net to hold it on the ground. Any obvious gaps in the hedges each side of the gate were earlier blocked. One man waited silently near the gate whilst his companion gently circled around to the other side of the field, accompanied sometimes by his dog, but only if it was well-disciplined, with a quiet nature and unlikely to bark. The man at the far side of the field would then walk towards the gate, making a noise so that the hares would run to escape through the apparent gaps in the gate. The net would fall as the stones were dislodged by the impact, and the waiting poacher would pounce on the entangled hare. If a suitable gate was not available, a similar procedure was carried out by placing nets to block the hares' traditional runs through gaps in the hedge. Other poachers caught hares by chasing them with their lurchers, the traditional gipsy poaching dog.

Shooting was also done but the procedure was risky because of the noise.

A favourite method to catch trout was by 'tickling'. The poacher lay down on his stomach on the river-bank, near a spot where the trout sheltered. He slowly immersed his arm in the water and waited patiently until a trout lingered. With great care and practice, it was possible to start tickling the trout on its underside with the fingers. When the gills came within the touch of his fingers, the poacher snatched his victim out of the water; the other parts of the fish were too slippery to hold.

Salmon were usually caught by netting, or sometimes grabbed out of shallow water with a gaff, when they were exhausted and resting after trying to fight their way upstream to spawn. The gaff consisted of a sturdy barbed hook with a hole in its metal base to which a thin rope was attached. The poacher would find or cut a suitable stick in the undergrowth to fit into the recess of the gaff-head. It was held firmly in position by pulling down on the rope and holding it tightly alongside the stick. The latter gave the rigidity and power for the poacher to strike the hook into the salmon. The stick was then allowed to fall away and the rope was used to pull the salmon to the bank. The head of the gaff was then hidden away, together with the salmon, and the poacher made his way home with no obvious sign of his illicit catch.

Nowadays, poaching has become extremely well organized, especially on salmon rivers. Fish are stunned with explosives or electrical devices and large nets are utilized to take hundreds of pounds' worth of fish in a few hours. The water bailiffs protecting the salmon have likewise become extremely professional in stalking the poachers. They wear camouflage, communicate with two-way radios, use night-sights to enhance their vision and carry powerful lamps which tend to dazzle a poacher like a rabbit caught in car headlights. The bailiffs never approach the poachers alone as sometimes resistance is encountered.

The poaching of deer has now also become widespread. It is often carried out under conditions of cruelty, using dogs, clubs, 'lamping' to freeze the quarry, and even automatic weapons. Unlike the solitary poacher who walked or later pedalled along on his bicycle, the commercial urban poachers travel long distances in motorized vehicles to steal their game. They often speed away from an area before it is even known that anything has been taken. The greed of the commercial poachers leads them to take game especially when stocks are low, as then high prices are obtained on the market. The approach of Christmas often brings an increase in poaching.

Deer stealing first became widespread at the beginning of the eighteenth century and continued right through the nineteenth century, with large gangs not only committing poaching offences but also damaging property and causing violent disturbances in their fights with the keepers. Rewards were offered to entice individuals to inform on their companions. The gamekeepers carried long staves to protect themselves in their fight against the poachers, who later started to carry arms. Gamekeepers also wore sturdy hats to shield their heads from the blows of cudgels wielded by their adversaries. The bowler hat was originally designed for just this purpose in 1850 by a Norfolk hatter. In Dorset, at Cranborne Chase the keepers donned padded jackets and beehive-shaped caps. They made their strange headgear from coils of twisted rolls of straw, bound together with split bramble runners. A tombstone near the north wall of Sixpenny Handley village conceals a hollow tomb formerly used by poachers to hide deer carcasses when they were being pursued by the keepers of the Chase.

Gangs in Waltham Chase in Hampshire carried out raids in aggressive style with blackened faces, to avoid recognition by the forest keepers in their night-time forays. The Waltham Black Act was passed in 1722 to combat such violence and poaching. The powers of the Act were far-reaching and introduced fifty new offences covering all aspects of poaching, from deer stealing at night to fish theft. Punishments were severe and anyone who offended twice was liable to transportation. Later, in 1755, it became an offence to sell game and this carried a penalty of a five pound fine or three months' imprisonment. £5 was the equivalent of £1,250 in today's terms.

When poachers started to use guns in the middle of the eighteenth century, a succession of further and even more severe Game Laws were initiated, in the second half of the century. An Act of 1770 imposed a prison sentence of six months for poaching at night. The penalties were made harsher by the 1773 Game Act, when daytime poaching carried a punishment of both flogging and a year's imprisonment. The payment of a large fine was an alternative but very few offenders could afford to pay. Nocturnal poaching carried the penalty of transportation for seven years. To protect further the landowners' game it became mandatory in 1784 for everyone hunting, fishing or shooting to possess a Game Certificate. The cost was two guineas a year for landowners and half a guinea for gamekeepers. William Pitt the Younger initiated the idea to raise extra duty, as part of his general policy of introducing new taxes and reviewing customs duties. The penalty for those caught without a certificate was a fine ranging from £20 to £50, or three months' imprisonment. By 1827 the number of Game Certificates issued had reached fifty thousand.

A law of 1803, called the Ellenborough Act, saw the introduction of possible capital punishment for poaching. Hanging was the penalty for carrying arms when poaching and resisting arrest. A further law of 1816 inflicted a punishment of seven years' transportation if a man was caught just carrying a net at night, even if he was unarmed. A humble cottager's attempt to take a hare or rabbit for his hungry dependants could result in a terrible family separation, leaving them in even greater poverty. As a consequence, many preferred to risk possible capital punishment by carrying arms to prevent arrest.

A series of Game Laws followed throughout the nineteenth century. There was no logical connection between them; they were introduced when a new need arose to protect the interests of the landowners and preserve their game. Some, such as the Ground Game Act 1880, were passed to alleviate anomalies and make concessions to the smaller farmers. Game protection was provided in the form of stipulated close seasons, banning of certain days and times within the permitted seasons, issuing of game licences and the imposition of various penalties for trespassers in search of game and theft.

The Night Poaching Act introduced in 1828 (later extended by the Night Poaching Act 1844) softened a little the dire consequences of poaching; for example, transportation was only imposed for a third offence, although an alternative sentence of two years' imprisonment with hard labour was sometimes given instead. A second offence carried the penalty of six months' imprisonment and the first offence three months, both with hard labour. The convicted person also had to find a surety to ensure that he did not offend again after release. If three or more persons acted together to poach, then the punishment was seven to fourteen years' transportation, or imprisonment with hard labour for three years. The Act granted powers to lawful occupiers of land, together with their servants, to apprehend suspected poachers on their property. If the offender offered physical resistance, then he was liable to be transported for seven years or imprisoned for two years with hard labour. The Night Poaching Act 1828 was applicable to enclosed and open land; and the extension of the Act in 1844 made it an offence to kill game or rabbits on any public road or path.

The Game Act 1831 defined in detail the game protected, including partridges, grouse, pheasants, hares, heath or moor game and black game. The eggs of the birds were also protected, together with those of wild swans, wild ducks, teal and widgeon. Close seasons were stipulated when it was illegal to kill the game. These were for partridges (1st February to 1st September), pheasants (1st February to 1st October), grouse (10th December to 12th August) and black game (10th December to 20th August). For the black game a variation was made for Somerset, Devon and the New Forest and the season was extended to 1st September. Outside the close seasons it was also illegal to kill game on Sundays and Christmas Day. The penalty was a fine of five pounds for each offence. The Game Act 1831 relaxed the severe restrictions of the earlier 1671 Act as regards who had the right to take game. The tenant of a piece of land was now allowed the privilege, as long as the landlord granted the right.

As well as the requirement of a game certificate to hunt or shoot, game could for the first time be sold to a licensed game dealer. The penalty for not possessing a game certificate or a licence to deal in game was a maximum fine of five pounds. Gamekeepers were given the power to arrest poachers found trespassing and seize any equipment such as guns, nets, snares, ferrets, etc. They were also given power to take game for the landowner at his request. However, all gamekeeper appointments had to be registered with the Clerk of the Peace. The harsh sentences for poaching were reduced; instead of possible transportation for a third offence of night poaching, the penalty became a prison sentence with hard labour. A convicted poacher was no longer flogged for his daytime misdemeanours but fined instead.

Further legislation followed, including The Hares Act 1848 and The Hares Preservation Act 1892. The former Act allowed persons, such as owners or occupiers of enclosed land, who had a right to kill hares in England and Wales to do so without a game certificate. The eventual consequence was a decrease in the number of hares and this resulted in the passing of The Hares Preservation Act 1892. This demanded a close season for hares during the breeding season from the beginning of March to the end of July. It was an offence to sell hares during this period and the penalty was a fine not to exceed twenty shillings.

The Game Licences Act 1860 reviewed the duties payable for game certificates and set a fee of six pounds, with a reduced fee of four pounds for a gamekeeper. The Royal Family were exempt. The Poaching Prevention Act 1862 granted power to police constables to search people, suspected of trespassing and poaching, without a warrant. The Act not only defined the game protected, such as hares, pheasants, partridges, woodcock, snipe, rabbits, grouse, black or moor game but also the eggs of the birds (with the exception of the woodcock and snipe). The Ground Game Act which came into force in 1880 was conciliatory to smaller farmers, as it permitted them to shoot hares and rabbits on the land they occupied. They were also exempted from having to have a game certificate but were prohibited from shooting at night. The Act was introduced to protect crops from damage by the ground game, defined as hares and rabbits.

The end of the nineteenth century and The Ground Game (Amendment) Act 1906 saw the continuation of the trend to less harsh sentences for poaching. It extended the right of occupiers of moorland to kill ground game between 1st September and 10th December inclusive. However, the Game Laws still provoked much friction between the classes. The Game Laws (Amendment) Act 1960 reduced the penalty for daytime poaching to a maximum fine of twenty pounds. If more than five people acted together, then the fine was fifty pounds. Despite this, the Act was designed to decrease the number of poaching offences. This was done by giving power to the police to enter land where poachers were suspected and to make arrests. They were allowed to search the suspect and seize any game, rabbits, guns, ammunition, snares and nets found in his possession. The Game Act 1970 amended the earlier Games Act 1831 to bring it up to date. The penalties stipulated in the various Game Acts have been amended many times since they were originally introduced. The current penalties in force for breaching the various statutes are now set by the Criminal Justice Act 1991. On a standard scale there are five levels of fines for different offences, the highest being five thousand pounds.

With regard to salmon, only licensed dealers were entitled to buy or sell the fish, as laid down by the Salmon Act 1986. It was also an offence to be in possession of a salmon not caught legally or to handle salmon in suspicious circumstances. The earlier Salmon and Freshwater Fisheries Act 1975 laid down regulations to protect fish generally and dealt with matters such as the prevention of obstructions impeding the free passage of fish in rivers, close seasons, trade in fish, licences, regulations for fisheries and the powers granted to water bailiffs to enforce the provisions of the Act. The close season for salmon was set from 31st October to 1st February and for trout, 30th September to 1st March. These standards could be varied by local river authorities.

The increase in the poaching of deer led to the Deer Act of 1963. This protected deer by imposing a close season and banning all killing at night. An exception was made during the close season for a landowner who needed to protect crops on his land from possible damage by deer during the daytime. The Act also banned inhumane methods of killing deer, such as the use of arrows, spears, nets and snares. The Theft Act 1968 stipulated a maximum fine of fifty pounds for the killing and unlawful taking of deer on enclosed land. A second offence warranted possible imprisonment up to three months, with a maximum fine of a hundred pounds. The Roe Deer (Close Seasons) Act 1977 was introduced to amend the Deer Act 1963, with respect to the close season for this species of deer. The Deer Act of 1980 gave additional protection to deer from poachers and restricted lawful trade in venison to licensed game dealers. Further protection came in more general form with the Wildlife and Countryside Act 1981 and the Wildlife and Countryside (Amendment) Act 1991.

The latest Deer Act 1991 repealed the previous ones and collated the legislation into one updated Act. Penalties were laid down for poaching and killing in the close season. These are, currently, imprisonment not exceeding three months, or a fine not exceeding £2,500; both may be imposed. If more than one deer were taken, then each was considered a separate offence. Exceptions were again made for occupiers of land when damage to crops or other property could occur. To ensure deer were only taken by humane methods the use of various weapons in addition to arrows, spears and snares was prohibited. These included the use of poisons, stupefying drugs or muscle-relaxing agents; smooth-bore shotguns and all forms of air-guns were banned. Rifles with a calibre greater than 0.240 inches were legal but only when fired with soft-nosed or hollow-nosed bullets. The close seasons when deer must not be killed were legislated as follows (all dates inclusive):

Red deer
Stags   1st May to 31st July
Hinds   1st March to 31st October

Fallow deer
Buck   1st May to 31st July
Doe   1st March to 31st October

Roe deer
Buck   1st November to 31st March
Doe   1st March to 31st October

Sika deer
Stags   1st May to 31st July
Hinds   1st March to 31st October

With regard to the shooting of game, there is no public right and permission must be obtained from the landowner who enjoys the shooting rights. Also, there is a strict control on firearms and the possession of a game certificate must always be accompanied by an authorized gun or shotgun certificate issued by the police. Anyone who trespasses carrying a firearm commits an offence under the Firearms Act 1968 and is liable to criminal prosecution for armed trespass.

Bibliography

Allen, N., *Exmoor's Wild Red Deer* (The Exmoor Press, 1990)

Batty, J., *Understanding Old English Game* (The Spur Publications Company, Hampshire 1976)

Beedell, S. (in association with B. Hargreaves), *The Complete Guide to Country Living* (David and Charles, 1979)

Bovill, E.W., *English Country Life 1780–1830* (Oxford University Press, 1962)

Brown, M., *The Royal Animals* (W.H. Allen, 1981)

Buxton, M., *Ladies of the Chase* (The Sportsman's Press, London 1987)

Carr, R., *English Fox Hunting* (Weidenfeld and Nicolson, 1986)

Chanin, P., *The Natural History of Otters* (Croom Helm, 1985)

Clayton, M., *The Chase. A Modern Guide to Fox Hunting* (Stanley Paul, 1987)

Corbet, G. and Harris, S., *The Handbook of British Mammals*, 3rd edition (Blackwell Scientific Publications, 1991)

Cowie, L.W., *A Dictionary of British Social History* (G. Bell and Sons, London 1973)

Cuddon, J.A., *The Macmillan Dictionary of Sports and Games* (The Macmillan Press, 1980)

Cuming, E.D., *British Sport Past and Present* (Hodder and Stoughton, 1909)

Cummins, J., *The Hound and The Hawk. The Art of Medieval Hunting* (Weidenfeld and Nicolson, 1988)

Cunliffe, J., *Popular Sight Hounds* (Popular Dogs Publishing Company, 1992)

Currie, L.W., *A Dictionary of British Social History* (G. Bell and Sons, 1973)

Glasier, P., *Falconry and Hawking* (B.T. Batsford, 1986)

Havins, P.J.N., *The Otter in Britain* (Robert Hale, 1981)

Hibbert, C., *The English. A Social History 1066–1945* (Grafton Books, 1987)

Holt, R., *Sport and the British. A Modern History* (Oxford University Press, 1989)

Hone, W., *The Every-Day Book Volumes 1 and 2* (William Tegg and Company, London 1824)

James, N.D.G., *A History of English Forestry* (Basil Blackwell, Oxford 1981)

Mallinson, J., *The Shadow of Extinction* (Macmillan, 1978)

Marchington, J., *The History of Wildfowling* (A & C Black Publishers, 1980)

Maurice, J.B., *Training Pointers and Setters* (David and Charles, 1974)

Mellanby, K., *Farming and Wildlife* (William Collins Sons and Company, 1981)

Mitchell, S., *The Dictionary of British Equestrian Arts* (Antique Collectors Club, 1985)

Niall, I., *The Poacher's Handbook* (William Heineman, 1950)

Page, R., *The Fox and the Orchid* (Quiller Press, London 1987)

Poole, R.W.F., *Hunting. An Introductory Handbook* (David and Charles, 1988)

Rickards, B., *Angling* (The Boydell Press, 1986)

Robinson, J.M., *The English Country Estate* (Century Hutchinson, 1988)

Trench, C.C., *A History of Marksmanship* (Longman, 1972)

Trench, C.C., *A History of Angling* (Hart-Davis, Macgibbon, 1974)

Trevelyan, G.M., *English Social History* (Longman Group, London 1978)

Turberville, A.S., *Johnson's England Volume 1* (Oxford University Press, 1967)

Upton, R., *Falconry Principles and Practice* (A & C Black Publishers, 1991)

Walton, I., *The Compleat Angler* (Harrap, London 1984)

Other books and publications

Book of the English Countryside (Drive Publications, 1988)

British Field Sports Society – Leaflets (BFSS, 59 Kennington Road, London SE1 7PZ)

League Against Cruel Sports – Leaflets (League Against Cruel Sports, 83–87 Union Street, London SE1 1SG)

Shakespeare's England Volume 2 (Clarendon Press, Oxford 1916)

Sporting Pastimes (ed. T. Curtis, Marshall Cavendish, 1990)

Steeplechasing and Foxhunting (ed. Michael Seth-Smith, New English Library, 1977)

The Agrarian History of England and Wales (Cambridge University Press, 1989)

The Book of Days Volumes 1 and 2 (ed. R. Chambers, W. and R. Chambers, London and Edinburgh 1864)

The Cambridge Guide to World Theatre (ed. Martin Banham, Cambridge University Press, 1988)

The Oxford Companion to Sports and Games (ed. J. Arlott, Oxford University Press, 1975)

Index